Mud and Kh

Sketches from Flanders and France

Vernon Bartlett

Alpha Editions

This edition published in 2023

ISBN : 9789357959476

Design and Setting By
Alpha Editions
www.alphaedis.com
Email - info@alphaedis.com

Contents

APOLOGIA

There has been so much written about the trenches, there are so many war photographs, so many cinema films, that one might well hesitate before even mentioning the war—to try to write a book about it is, I fear, to incur the censure of the many who are tired of hearing about bombs and bullets, and who prefer to read of peace, and games, and flirtations.

But, for that very reason, I venture to think that even so indifferent a war book as mine will not come entirely amiss. When the Lean Years are over, when the rifle becomes rusty, and the khaki is pushed away in some remote cupboard, there is great danger that the hardships of the men in the trenches will too soon be forgotten. If, to a minute extent, anything in these pages should help to bring home to people what war really is, and to remind them of their debt of gratitude, then these little sketches will have justified their existence.

Besides, I am not entirely responsible for this little book. Not long ago, I met a man—fit, single, and young—who began to grumble to me of the hardships of his "funkhole" in England, and, incidentally, to belittle the hardships of the man at the front. After I had told him exactly what I thought of him, I was still so indignant that I came home and began to write a book about the trenches. Hence *Mud and Khaki*. To him, then, the blame for this minor horror of war. I wash my hands of it.

And I try to push the blame off on to him, for I realise that I have undertaken an impossible task—the most practised pen cannot convey a real notion of the life at the front, as the words to describe war do not exist. Even you who have lost your husbands and brothers, your fathers and sons, can have but the vaguest impression of the cruel, thirsty claws that claimed them as victims. First must you see the shattered cottages of France and Belgium, the way in which the women clung to their homes in burning Ypres, the long streams of refugees wheeling their poor little *lares et penates*, their meagre treasures, on trucks and handcarts; first must you listen to the cheery joke that the Angel of Death finds on the lips of the soldier, to the songs that encourage you in the dogged marches through the dark and the mud, to the talk during the long nights when the men collect round the brazier fire and think of their wives and kiddies at home, of murky streets in the East End, of quiet country inns where the farmers gather of an evening.

No words, then, can give an exact picture of these things, but they may help to give colour to your impressions. Heaven forbid that, by telling the horrors of war, the writers of books should make pessimists of those at home! Heaven forbid that they should belittle the dangers and hardships, and so take away some of the glory due to "Tommy" for all he has suffered for the Motherland! There is a happy mean—the men at the front have found it; they know that death is near, but they can still laugh and sing.

In these sketches and stories I have tried, with but little success, to keep that happy mean in view. If the pictures are very feeble in design when compared to the many other, and far better, works on the same subject, remember, reader, that the intention is good, and accept this apology for wasting your time.

A few of these sketches and articles have already appeared elsewhere. My best thanks are due to the Editors of the *Daily Mail* and the *Daily Mirror* for their kind permission to include several sketches which appeared, in condensed forms, in their papers. I am also grateful to the Editor of Cassell's *Storyteller* for his permission to reproduce "The Knut," which first saw print in that periodical.

VERNON BARTLETT.

I

IN HOSPITAL

Close behind the trenches on the Ypres salient stands part of "Chapel Farm"—the rest of it has long been trampled down into the mud by the many hundreds of men who have passed by there. Enough of the ruin still stands for you to trace out the original plan of the place—a house and two barns running round three sides of the farmyard that is fœtid and foul and horrible.

It is an uninviting spot, for, close by, are the remains of a dead cow, superficially buried long ago by some working party that was in a hurry to get home; but the farm is notable for the fact that passing round the north side of the building you are out of view, and safe, and that passing round the south side you can be seen by the enemy, and are certain to be sniped.

If you must be sniped, however, you might choose a worse place, for the bullets generally fly low there, and there is a cellar to which you can be carried—a filthy spot, abounding in rats, and damp straw, and stained rags, for the place once acted as a dressing-station. But still, it is under cover, and intact, with six little steps leading up into the farmyard.

And one day, as I led a party of men down to the "dumping ground" to fetch ammunition, I was astonished to hear the familiar strains of "Gilbert the Filbert" coming from this desolate ruin. The singer had a fine voice, and he gave forth his chant as happily as though he were safe at home in England, with no cares or troubles in the world. With a sergeant, I set out to explore; as our boots clattered on the cobble-stones of the farmyard, there was a noise in the cellar, a head poked up in the entrance, and I was greeted with a cheery "Good morning, sir."

We crawled down the steps into the hovel to learn the singer's story. He was a man from another regiment, who had come down from his support dug-out to "nose around after a spud or two." The German sniper had "bagged" him in the ankle and he had crawled into the cellar—still with his sandbag of "spuds"—to wait until someone came by. "I 'adn't got nothing to do but wait," he concluded, "and if I'd got to wait, I might jest as well play at bein' a bloomin' canary as 'owl like a kid what's 'ad it put acrost 'im."

We got a little water from the creaky old pump and took off his "first field dressing" that he had wound anyhow round his leg. To my surprise—for he was so cheerful that I thought he had only a scratch—I found that his ankle was badly smashed, and that part of his boot and sock had been driven right into the wound.

"Yes, it did 'urt a bit when I tried to walk," he said, as I expressed surprise. "That's jest the best part of it. I don't care if it 'urts like 'ell, for it's sure to mean 'Blighty' and comfort for me."

And that is just the spirit of the hospitals—the joy of comfort and rest overbalances the pain and the operation. To think that there are still people who imagine that hospitals are of necessity sad and depressing! Why, even the children's wards of the London Hospital are not that, for, as you look down the rows of beds, you see surprise and happiness on the poor little pinched faces—surprise that everything is clean and white, and that they are lying between proper sheets; happiness that they are treated kindly, and that there are no harsh words. As for a military hospital, while war lays waste the world, there is no place where there is more peace and contentment.

Hospital, for example, is the happiest place to spend Christmas. About a week before the day there are mysterious whispers in the corners, and furtive writing in a notebook, and the clinking of coppers. Then, next day, a cart comes to the door and deposits a load of ivy and holly and mistletoe. The men have all subscribed to buy decorations for their temporary home, and they set about their work like children—for where will you find children who are younger than the "Tommies"? Even the wards where there are only "cot cases" are decorated, and the men lie in bed and watch the invaders from other wards who come in and smother the place with evergreens. There is one ward where a man lies dying of cancer—here, too, they come, making clumsy attempts to walk on tip-toe, and smiling encouragement as they hang the mistletoe from the electric light over his bed.

And at last the great day comes. There are presents for everyone, and a bran pie from which, one by one, they extract mysterious parcels wrapped up in brown paper. And the joy as they undo them! There are table games and packets of tobacco, writing pads and boxes of cigarettes, cheap fountain pens which will nearly turn the Matron's hair grey, and bags of chocolates. They collect in their wards and turn their presents over, their eyes damp with joy; they pack up their games or their chocolate to send home to their wives who are spending Christmas in lonely cottage kitchens; they write letters to imaginary people just for the joy of using their writing blocks; they admire each others' treasures, and, sometimes, make exchanges, for the man who does not smoke has drawn a pipe, and the man in the corner over there, who has lost both legs, has drawn a pair of felt slippers!

Before they know where they are, the lunch is ready, and, children again, they eat far more than is good for them, until the nurses have to forbid them to have any more. "No, Jones," they say, "you can't have a third helping of pudding; you're supposed to be on a milk diet."

Oh, the happiness of it all! All day they sing and eat and talk, until you forget that there is war and misery in the world; when the evening comes they go, flushed and happy, back to their beds to dream that great black Germans are sitting on them, eating Christmas puddings by the dozen, and growing heavier with each one.

But upstairs in the little ward the mother sits with her son, and she tries with all her force to keep back the tears. They have had the door open all day to hear the laughter and fun, and on the table by the bed lie his presents and the choicest fruit and sweets. Until quite late at night she stays there, holding her son's hand, and telling of Christmases when he was a little boy. Then, when she gets up to go, the man in bed turns his head towards the poor little pile of presents. "You'd better take those, mother," he says. "They won't be much use to me. But it's the happiest Christmas I've ever had." And all the poor woman's courage leaves her, and she stoops forward under the mistletoe and kisses him, kisses him, with tears streaming down her face.

Most stirring of all are the clearing hospitals near the firing line. They are crowded, and all night long fresh wounded stumble in, the mud caked on their uniforms, and their bandages soiled by dark stains. In one corner a man groans unceasingly: "Oh, my head ... God! Oh, my poor head!" and you hear the mutterings and laughter of the delirious.

But if the pain here is at its height, the relief is keenest. For months they have lived in hell, these men, and now they have been brought out of it all. A man who has been rescued from suffocation in a coal mine does not grumble if he has the toothache; a man who has come from the trenches and death does not complain of the agony of his wound—he smiles because he is in comfortable surroundings for once.

Besides, there is a great feeling of expectation and hope, for there is to be a convoy in the morning and they are all to be sent down to the base—all except the men who are too ill to be moved and the two men who have died in the night, whose beds are shut off by red screens. The "cot cases" are lifted carefully on to stretchers, their belongings are packed under their pillows, and they are carried down to the ambulances, while the walking cases wander about the wards, waiting for their turn to come. They look into their packs for the fiftieth time to make sure they have left nothing; they lean out of the windows to watch the ambulance roll away to the station; they stop every orderly who comes along to ask if they have not been forgotten, or if there will be room for them on the train; they make new acquaintances, or discover old ones. One man meets a long-lost friend with a huge white bandage round his neck. "Hullo, you poor devil," he says, "how did you get it in the neck like that? was it a bullet or a bit of a shell?" The other swears, and confesses that he has not been hit at all, but is suffering from boils.

For, going down to the base are wounded and sick of every sort—men who have lost a limb, and men who have only the tiniest graze; men who are mad with pain, and men who are going down for a new set of false teeth; men with pneumonia, and men with scabies. It is only when the boat leaves for England that the cases can be sorted out. It is only then that there are signs of envy, and the men whose wounds are not bad enough to take them back to "Blighty" curse because the bullet did not go deeper, or the bit of shrapnel did not touch the bone.

It is a wonderful moment for the "Tommies" when they reach their convalescent hospital in England. Less than a week ago many of them were stamping up and down in a slushy trench wondering "why the 'ell there's a bloomin' war on at all." Less than a week ago many of them never thought to see England again, and now they are being driven up to the old Elizabethan mansion that is to be their hospital.

As the ambulance draws up outside the porch, the men can see, where the hostess used to welcome her guests of old, the matron waiting with the medical officer to welcome them in. One by one they are brought into the oak-panelled hall, and a nurse stoops over them to read their names, regiments, and complaints off the little labels that are fastened to their tunic buttons. As they await their turns, they snuff the air and sigh happily, they talk, and wink, and smile at the great carved ceiling, and forget all they have gone through in the joy of that splendid moment.

Away in one of the wards a gramophone is playing "Mother Machree," and the little nurse, who hums the tune to herself as she leans over each man to see his label, sees a tear crawling through the grey stubble on one's cheek. He is old and Irish, and had not hoped to hear Irish tunes and to see fair women again. But he is ashamed of his emotion, and he tells a little lie. "Sure, an' it's rainin' outside, nurse," he says.

And the nurse, who knows the difference between a raindrop and a tear—for was she not standing on the step five minutes ago, admiring the stars and the moon?—knows her part well, and plays it. "I thought I heard the rain dripping down on the porch just now," she says, "I hope you poor men did not get wet," and she goes on to her next patient.

How they love those days in hospital! How the great rough men love to be treated like babies, to be petted and scolded, ordered about and praised! How grand it is to see the flowers, to feel one's strength returning, to go for drives and walks, to find a field that is not pitted by shell holes! And how cheerful they all are, these grown-up babies!

The other day I opened the door of the hospital and discovered a "convoy" consisting of three legless and two armless men, trying to help each other up the six low steps, and shouting with laughter at their efforts. And one of them saw the pity on my face, for he grinned.

"Don't you worry about us," he said. "I wouldn't care if I 'ad no arms nor eyes nor legs, so long as I was 'ome in Blighty again. Why"—and his voice dropped as he let me into the secret—"I've 'ad a li'l boy born since I went out to the front, an' I never even seed the li'l beggar yet. Gawd, we in 'orspital is the lucky ones, an' any bloke what ain't killed ought to be 'appy and bright like what we is."

And it is the happiness of all these men that makes hospital a very beautiful place, for nowhere can you find more courage and cheerfulness than among these fellows with their crutches and their bandages.

There was only one man—Bill Stevens—who seemed despondent and miserable, and we scarcely wondered—he was blind, and lay in bed day after day, with a bandage round his head, the only blind man in the hospital. He was silent and morbid, and would scarcely mutter a word of thanks when some man came right across the ward on his crutches to do him a trifling service, but he had begged to be allowed to stay in the big ward until the time came for him to go off to a special hostel for the men who have lost their sight. And the men who saw him groping about helplessly in broad daylight forgave him his surliness, and ceased to wonder at his despondency.

But even Bill Stevens was to change, for there came a day when he received a letter.

"What's the postmark?" he demanded.

"Oxford," said the nurse. "Shall I read it to you?"

But Bill Stevens clutched his letter tight and shook his head, and it was not until lunch-time that anything more was heard of it. Then he called the Sister to him, and she read the precious document almost in a whisper, so secret was it. Private Bill Stevens plucked nervously at the bedclothes as the Sister recited the little love sentences:—How was dear Bill? Why hadn't he told his Emily what was wrong with him? That she, Emily, would come to see him at four o'clock that afternoon, and how nice it would be.

"Now you keep quiet and don't worry," said the Sister, "or you'll be too ill to see her. Why, I declare that you're quite feverish. What have you got to worry about?"

"You see, it's like this 'ere," confided Bill Stevens. "I ain't dared to tell 'er as 'ow I was blind, and it ain't fair to ask 'er to marry a bloke what's 'elpless. She only thinks I've got it slightly, and she won't care for me any more now."

"You needn't be frightened," said the Sister. "If she's worth anything at all, she'll love you all the more now." And she tucked him up and told him to go to sleep.

Then, when Emily arrived, the Sister met her, and broke the news. "You love him, don't you?" she asked, and Emily blushed, and smiled assent through her tears.

"Then," said the Sister, "do your best to cheer him up. Don't let him think you're distressed at his blindness," and she took the girl along to the ward where Bill Stevens lay waiting, restless and feverish.

"Bill darling," said Emily. "It's me. How are you? Why have you got that bandage on?" But long before poor Bill could find words to break the news to her she stooped over him and whispered: "Bill dear, I could almost wish you were blind, so that you'd have to depend on me, like. If it wasn't for your own pain, I'd wish you was blind, I would really."

For a long time Bill stuttered and fumbled for words, for his joy was too great. "I am blind, Em'ly," he murmured at last.

And the whole ward looked the other way as Emily kissed away his fears. As for Bill Stevens, he sang and laughed and talked so much that evening that the Matron had to come down to stop him.

For, as my legless friend remarked, "We in 'orspital is the lucky ones, an' any bloke what ain't killed ought to be 'appy and bright like we is."

II

A RECIPE FOR GENERALS

Everyone is always anxious to get on the right side of his General; I have chanced upon a recipe which I believe to be infallible for anyone who wears spurs, and who can, somehow or other, get himself in the presence of that venerated gentleman.

I sat one day in a trench outside my dug-out, eating a stew made of bully beef, ration biscuits, and foul water. Inside my dug-out, the smell of buried men was not conducive to a good appetite; outside, some horrible Hun was amusing himself by firing at the sandbag just above me, and sending showers of earth down my neck and into my food. It is an aggravating fact that the German always makes himself particularly objectionable about lunch-time, and that, whenever you go in the trench, his bullets seem to follow you—an unerring instinct brings them towards food. A larger piece of earth than usual in my stew routed the last vestige of my good-humour. Prudence warning me of the futility of losing my temper with a Hun seventy yards away, I called loudly for my servant.

"Jones," I said, when he came up, "take away this stuff. It's as bad as a gas attack. I'm fed up with it. I'm fed up with Maconochie, I'm fed up with the so-called 'fresh' meat that sometimes makes its appearance. Try to get hold of something new; give me a jugged hare, or a pheasant, or something of that kind."

"Yessir," said Jones, and he hurried off round the traverse to finish my stew himself.

It never does to speak without first weighing one's words. This is an old maxim—I can remember something about it in one of my first copy-books; but, like most other maxims, it is never learnt in real life. My thoughtless allusion to "jugged hare" set my servant's brain working, for hares and rabbits have, before now, been caught behind the firing line. The primary difficulty, that of getting to the country haunted by these animals, was easily solved, for, though an officer ought not to allow a man to leave a trench without a very important reason, the thought of new potatoes at a ruined farm some way back, or cherries in the orchard, generally seems a sufficiently important reason to send one's servant back on an errand of pillage. Thus it was that, unknown to me, my servant spent part of the next three days big-game hunting behind the firing line.

My first intimation of trouble came to me the day after we had gone back to billets for a rest, when an orderly brought me a message from Brigade Headquarters. It ran as follows:—

"Lieut. Newcombe is to report at Brigade Headquarters this afternoon at 2 p.m. to furnish facts with reference to his servant, No. 6789, Pte. Jones W., who, on the 7th inst., discharged a rifle behind the firing line, to the great personal danger of the Brigadier, Pte. Jones's Company being at the time in the trenches.

"(*Signed*) G. MACKINNON,
"*Brigade Major.*"

"Jones," I cried, "come and explain this to me," and I read him the incriminating document.

My servant's English always suffers when he is nervous.

"Well, sir," he began, "it 'appened like this 'ere. After what you said the other day abaht bully beef, I went orf ter try ter git a rabbit or an 'are. I seen sev'ral, sir, but I never 'it one nor wired one. Then, on Friday, jest as I was shootin' at an 'ole 'are what I see, up kime an orficer, one o' thim Staff gints. 'Who are you?' 'e asks. I told 'im as I was a servant, and was jest tryin' ter git an 'are fer my bloke—beggin' yer pardon, sir, I mean my orficer. Then, after a lot more talk, 'e says, 'Do yer know that yer gone and nearly 'it the Gen'ril?' That's all as I knows abaht it, sir. I never wanted ter 'it no Gen'ril."

"All this, and not even a rabbit!" I sighed. "It's a serious business, and you ought to have known better than to go letting off ammunition behind the firing line. However, I'll see what can be done," and my servant went away, rather crestfallen, to drown his sorrows in a glass of very mild, very unpleasant Belgian beer.

An hour or two later, I strolled across to a neighbouring billet to see a friend, and to tell him of my coming interview.

"You'll get hell," was his only comfort. Then, as an afterthought, he said, "You'd better wear my spurs; they'll help to impress him. A clink of spurs will make even your salute seem smart."

Thus it was that I, who am no horseman, rode over to Brigade Headquarters, a mile away, with my toes turned in, and a pair of bright and shining spurs turned away as far as possible from my horse's flanks.

Unhappy and ill at ease, I was shown into the General's room.

"Mr. Newcombe," he began, after a preliminary glance at a paper in front of him, "this is a very serious matter. It is a serious offence on the part of Private Jones, who, I understand, is your servant."

"Yes, sir."

"It is also an example of gross carelessness on your part."

"Yes, sir."

"I was returning from the trenches on your right on Friday last, when a bullet flew past my head, coming from the direction opposed to the Germans. I have a strong objection to being shot at by my own men, right behind the fire trenches, so I sent Captain Neville to find out who had fired, and he found your servant."

"Yes, sir."

"Well, can you give any explanation of this extraordinary event?"

I explained to the best of my ability.

"It is a very unusual case," said the General, when I had finished. "I do not wish to pursue the matter further, as you are obviously the real person to blame."

"Yes, sir."

"I am very dissatisfied about it, and you must please see that better discipline is kept. I do not like to proceed against officers under my command, so the matter drops here. You must reprimand your servant very severely, and, I repeat, I am very dissatisfied. You may go, Mr."—here another glance at the paper before him—"Newcombe. Good afternoon."

I brought my heels together for a very smart salute ... and locked my spurs! For some seconds I stood swaying helplessly in front of him, then I toppled forward, and, supporting myself with both hands upon his table, I at length managed to separate my feet. When I ventured to look at him again to apologise, I saw that his frown had gone, and his mouth was twitching in a strong inclination to laugh.

"You are not, I take it, Mr. Newcombe, quite accustomed to wearing spurs?" he said presently.

I blushed horribly, and, in my confusion, blurted out my reason for putting them on. This time he laughed unrestrainedly. "Well, you have certainly impressed me with them." Then, just as I was preparing to go, he said, "Will you have a glass of whisky, Newcombe, before you go? Neville," he called to the Staff Captain in the next room, "you might ask Andrews to bring the whisky and some glasses."

"Good afternoon," said the General, very affably, when, after a careful salute, I finally took my leave.

Let anyone who will try this recipe for making friends with a General. I do not venture to guarantee its infallibility, however, for that depends entirely on the General himself, and, to such, rules and instruction do not apply.

III

"MUD!"

Those at home in England, with their experience of war books and photographs, of Zeppelin raids and crowded hospitals, are beginning to imagine they know all there is to know about war. The truth is that they still have but little idea of the life in the trenches, and, as far as mud is concerned, they are delightfully ignorant. They do not know what mud is.

They have read of Napoleon's "Fourth Element," they have listened to long descriptions of mud in Flanders and France, they have raised incredulous eyebrows at tales of men being drowned in the trenches, they have given a fleeting thought of pity for the soldiers "out there" as they have slushed home through the streets on rainy nights; but they have never realised what mud means, for no photograph can tell its slimy depth, and even the pen of a Zola or a Victor Hugo could give no adequate idea of it.

And so, till the end of the war, the old story will be continued—while the soldier flounders and staggers about in that awful, sucking swamp, the pessimist at home will lean back in his arm-chair and wonder, as he watches the smoke from his cigar wind up towards the ceiling, why we do not advance at the rate of one mile an hour, why we are not in Berlin, and whether our army is any good at all. If such a man would know why we are not in German territory, let him walk, on a dark night, through the village duck-pond, and then sleep in his wet clothes in the middle of the farmyard. He would still be ignorant of mud and wet, but he would cease to wonder and grumble.

It is the infantryman who suffers most, for he has to live, eat, sleep, and work in the mud. The plain of dragging slime that stretches from Switzerland to the sea is far worse to face than the fire of machine guns or the great black trench-mortar bombs that come twisting down through the air. It is more terrible than the frost and the rain—you cannot even stamp your feet to drive away the insidious chill that mud always brings. Nothing can keep it from your hands and face and clothes; there is no taking off your boots to dry in the trenches—you must lie down just as you are, and often you are lucky if you have two empty sandbags under you to save you from the cold embrace of the swamp.

But if the mud stretch is desolate by day, it is shocking by night. Imagine a battalion going up to the trenches to relieve another regiment. The rain comes beating pitilessly down on the long trail of men who stumble along in the blackness over the *pavé*. They are all well loaded, for besides his pack, rifle, and equipment, each man carries a pick or a bag of rations or a bundle of firewood. At every moment comes down the line the cry to "keep to the right," and the whole column stumbles off the *pavé* into the deep mud by the roadside to allow the passage of an ambulance or a transport waggon. There is no smoking, for they are too close to the enemy, and there is the thought of six days and six nights of watchfulness and wetness in the trenches.

Presently the winding line strikes off the road across the mud. This is not mud such as we know it in England—it is incredibly slippery and impossibly tenacious, and each dragging footstep calls for a tremendous effort. The men straggle, or close up together so that they have hardly the room to move; they slip, and knock into each other, and curse; they are hindered by little ditches, and by telephone wires that run, now a few inches, now four or five feet from the ground. One man trips over an old haversack that is lying in his path—God alone knows how many haversacks and how many sets of equipment have been swallowed up by the mud on the plain of Flanders, part of the equipment of the wounded that has been thrown aside to lighten the burden—and when he scrambles to his feet again he is a mass of mud, his rifle barrel is choked with it, it is in his hair, down his neck, everywhere. He staggers on, thankful only that he did not fall into a shell hole, when matters would have been much worse.

Just when the men are waiting in the open for the leading platoon to file down into the communication trench, a German star shell goes up, and a machine gun opens fire a little farther down the line. As the flare sinks down behind the British trench it lights up the white faces of the men, all crouching down in the swamp, while the bullets swish by, "like a lot of bloomin' swallers," above their heads.

And now comes the odd quarter of a mile of communication trench. It is very narrow, for the enemy can enfilade it, and it is paved with brushwood and broken bricks, and a little drain, that is meant to keep the floor dry, runs along one side of it. In one place a man steps off the brushwood into the drain, and he falls headlong. The others behind have no time to stop themselves, and a grotesque pile of men heaps itself up in the narrow, black trench. One man laughing, the rest swearing, they pick themselves up again, and tramp on to the firing line.

Here the mud is even worse than on the plain they have crossed. All the engineers and all the trench pumps in the world will not keep a trench decently dry when it rains for nine hours in ten and when the trench is the lowest bit of country for miles around. The men can do nothing but "carry on"—the parapet must be kept in repair whatever the weather; the sandbags must be filled however wet and sticky the earth. The mud may nearly drag a man's boot off at his every step—indeed, it often does; but the man must go on digging, shovelling, lining the trench with tins, logs, bricks, and planks in the hope that one day he may have put enough flooring into the trench to reach solid ground beneath the mud.

All this, of course, is only the infantryman's idea of things. From a tactical point of view mud has a far greater importance—it is the most relentless enemy that an army can be called upon to face. Even without mud and without Germans it would be a very difficult task to feed and look after a million men on the move; with these two discomforts movement becomes almost impossible.

It is only after you have seen a battery of field artillery on the move in winter that you can realise at all the enormous importance of good weather when an advance is to be made. You must watch the horses labouring and plunging in mud that reaches nearly to their girths; you must see the sweating, half-naked men striving, with outstanding veins, to force the wheels round; you must hear the sucking cry of the mud when it slackens its grip; and you must remember that this is only a battery of light guns that is being moved.

It is mud, then, that is the great enemy. It is the mud, then, and not faulty organisation or German prowess that you must blame if we do not advance as fast as you would like. Even if we were not to advance another yard in another year, people in England should not be disheartened. "Out there" we are facing one of the worst of foes. If we do not advance, or if we advance too slowly, remember that it is mud that is the cause—not the German guns.

IV

THE SURPRISE ATTACK

"Do you really feel quite fit for active service again?" asked the President of the Medical Board.

It was not without reason that Roger Dymond hesitated before he gave his answer, for nerves are difficult things to deal with. It is surprising, but it is true, that you never find a man who is afraid the first time he goes under fire. There are thousands who are frightened beforehand—frightened that they will "funk it" when the time comes, but when they see men who have been out for months "ducking" as each shell passes overhead they begin to think what brave fellows they are, and they wonder what fear is. But after they have been in the trenches for weeks, when they realise what a shell can do, their nerve begins to go; they start when they hear a rifle fired, and they crouch down close to the ground at the whistle of a passing shell.

Thus had it been with Roger Dymond. At the beginning of the war he had enjoyed himself—if anyone could enjoy that awful retreat and awful advance. He had been one of the first officers to receive the Military Cross, for brilliant work by the canal at Givenchy; he had laughed and joked as he lay all day in the open and listened to the bullets that went "pht" against the few clods of earth he had erected with his entrenching tool, and which went by the high-sounding name of "head cover."

And then, one day a howitzer shell had landed in the dug-out where he was lunching with his three particular friends. When the men of his company cleared the sandbags away from him, he was a gibbering wreck, unwounded but paralysed, and splashed with the blood of three dead men.

Now, after months of battle dreams and mad terror, of massage and electrical treatment, he was faced with the question—"Do you feel quite fit for active service again?"

He was tired to death of staying at home with no apparent complaint, he was sick of light duty with his reserve battalion, he wanted to be out at the front again with the men and officers he knew ... and yet, supposing his nerve went again, supposing he lost his self-control....

Finally, however, he looked up. "Yes, sir," he said, "I feel fit for anything now—quite fit."

Three months later the Medical Officer sat talking to the C.O. in the Headquarter dug-out.

"As for old Dymond," he said, "he ought never to have been sent out here again. He's done his bit already, and they ought to have given him a 'cushy' job at home, instead of one of those young staff blighters"—for the M.O. was no respecter of persons, and even a "brass hat" failed to awe him.

"Can't you send him down the line?" said the C.O. "This is no place for a man with neurasthenia. God! did you see the way his hand shook when he was in here just now?"

"And he's a total abstainer now, poor devil," sighed the Doctor with pity, for he was, himself, fond of his drop of whisky. "I'll send him down to the dressing station to-morrow with a note telling the R.A.M.C. people there that he wants a thorough change."

"Good," said the C.O. "I'm very sorry he's got to go, for he's a jolly good officer. However, it can't be helped. Have another drink, Doc."

It is bad policy to refuse the offer of a senior officer, and the M.O. was a man with a thirst, so he helped himself with liberality. Before he had raised the glass to his lips, the sudden roar of many bursting shells caused him to jump to his feet. "Hell!" he growled. "Another hate. More dirty work at the cross roads." And he hurried off to the little dug-out that served him as a dressing station, his beloved drink standing untouched on the table.

Meanwhile, Roger Dymond crouched up against the parapet, and listened to the explosions all around him. "Oil cans" and "Minnewerfer" bombs came hurtling through the air, "Crumps" burst with great clouds of black smoke, bits of "Whizz-bangs" went buzzing past and buried themselves deep in the ground. Roger Dymond tried to light his cigarette, but his hand shook so that he could hardly hold the match, and he threw it away in fear that the men would see how he trembled.

Thousands of people have tried to describe the noise of a shell, but no man can know what it is like unless he can put himself into a trench to hear the original thing. There is the metallic roar of waves breaking just before the rain, there is the whistle of wind through the trees, there is the rumble of a huge traction engine, and there is the sharp back-fire of a motor car. With each different sinister noise, Roger Dymond felt his hold over himself gradually going ... going....

Next to him in the trench crouched Newman, a soldier who had been in his platoon in the old days when they tramped, sweating and half-dead, along the broiling roads towards Paris.

"They'm a blasted lot too free with their iron crosses and other souvenirs," growled that excellent fellow. "I'd rather be fighting them 'and to 'and like we did in that there churchyard near Le Cateau, wouldn't you, sir?"

Dymond smiled sickly assent, and Newman, being an old soldier, knew what was the matter with his captain. He watched him as, bit by bit, his nerve gave way, but he dared not suggest that Dymond should "go sick," and he did the only thing that could be done under the circumstances—he talked as he had never talked before.

"Gawd!" he said after a long monologue that was meant to bring distraction from the noise of the inferno. "I wish as 'ow we was a bit closer to the devils so that they couldn't shell us. I'd like to get me 'and round some blighter's ugly neck, too."

A second later a trench-mortar bomb came hurtling down through the air, and fell on the parados near the two men. There was a pause, then an awful explosion, which hurled Dymond to the ground, and, as he fell, Newman's words seemed to run through his head: "I wish as 'ow we was a bit closer to the devils so that they couldn't shell us." He was aware of a moment's acute terror, then something in his brain seemed to snap and everything that followed was vague, for Captain Roger Dymond went mad.

He remembered clambering out of the trench to get so close to the Huns that they could not shell him; he remembered running—everybody running, his own men running with him, and the Germans running from him; he had a vague recollection of making his way down a long bit of strange trench, brandishing an entrenching tool that he had picked up somewhere; then there was a great flash and an awful pain, and all was over—the shelling was over at last.

It was not until Roger Dymond was in hospital in London that he worried about things again. One evening, however, the Sister brought in a paper, and pointed out his own name in a list of nine others who had won the V.C. He read the little paragraph underneath in the deepest astonishment.

"For conspicuous gallantry," it ran, "under very heavy shell fire on August 26th, 1916. Seeing that his men were becoming demoralised by the bombardment, Captain Dymond, on his own initiative, led a surprise attack against the enemy trenches. He found the Germans unprepared, and at the head of his men captured two lines of trenches along a front of two hundred and fifty yards. Captain Dymond lost both legs owing to shell fire, but his men were able to make good almost all their ground and to hold it against all counter-attacks.

"This officer was awarded the Military Cross earlier in the war for great bravery near La Bassée."

He finished the amazing article, and wrote a letter, in a wavering hand that he could not recognise as his own, to the War Office to tell them of their mistake—that he was really running away from the enemy's shells—and received a reply visit from a general.

"My dear fellow," he said, "the V.C. is never awarded to a man who has not deserved it. The only pity is that so many fellows deserve it and don't get it. You deserved it and got it. Stick to it, and think yourself damned lucky to be alive to wear it. There's nothing more to be said."

And this is the story of Captain Roger Dymond, V.C., M.C. Of the few of us who were there at the time, there is not one who would grudge him the right to put those most coveted letters of all after his name, for we were all in the shelling ourselves, and we all saw him charge, and heard him shout and laugh as he made his way across to the enemy. The V.C., as the general said, is never given to a man who has not deserved it.

V

"PONGO" SIMPSON ON BOMBS

"Pongo" Simpson was sitting before a brazier fire boiling some tea for his captain, when the warning click sounded from the German trenches. Instinctively he clapped the cover on the canteen and dived for shelter, while the great, black trench-mortar bomb came twisting and turning down through the air. It fell to ground with a dull thud, there was a second's silence, then an appalling explosion. The roof of the dug-out in which "Pongo" had found refuge sagged ominously, the supporting beam cracked, and the heavy layer of earth and bricks and branches subsided on the crouching man.

It took five minutes to dig him out, and he was near to suffocation when they dragged him into the trench. For a moment he looked wonderingly about him, and then a smile came to his face. "That's what I likes about this 'ere life, there ain't no need to get bored. No need for pictcher shows or pubs, there's amusements for you for nothing." And as he got to his feet, a scowl replaced the smile. "I bet I knows the blighter what sent that there bomb," he growled. "I guess it's old Fritz what used to 'ang out in that old shop in Walworth Road—'im what I palmed off a bad 'arf-crown on. 'E always said as 'ow 'e'd get 'is own back."

Five minutes later he had exchanged the battered wreck of his canteen for a new one belonging to Private Adams, who was asleep farther down the trench, and had set to boiling a fresh lot of tea for his captain.

"Darned funny things, bombs and things like that," he began presently. "You can't trust them no'ow. Look at ole Sergeant Allen f'r example. 'E went 'ome on leave after a year out 'ere, and 'e took an ornary time fuse from a shell with 'im to put on 'is mantelpiece. And the very first night as 'e was 'ome, the blamed thing fell down when 'e wasn't lookin', and bit 'im in the leg, so that 'e 'ad to spend all 'is time in 'orspital. They're always explodin' when they didn't ought to. Did I ever tell you about me brother Bert?"

A chorus in the negative from the other men who stood round the brazier encouraged him to continue.

"Well, Bert was always a bit silly like, and I thought as 'ow 'e'd do somethin' foolish when 'e got to the front. Sure 'nough, the very first bloomin' night 'e went into a trench, 'e was filin' along it when 'e slipped and sat right on a box of bombs. It's gorspel what I'm tellin' you—nine of the blighters went off, and 'e wasn't killed. 'E's 'ome in England now in some 'orspital, and 'e's as fit as a lord. The only thing wrong about 'im now is that 'e's always the first bloke what stands and gives 'is place to a lady when a tram's full—still a bit painful like."

Joe Bates expectorated with much precision and care over the parapet in the direction of the Germans. "It ain't bombs wot I mind," he said, "it's them there mines. When I first kime aht ter fight the 'Uns, I was up at St. Eloi, an' they blew the 'ole lot of us up one night. Gawd, it ain't like nothin' on earth, an' the worst of it was I'd jest 'ad a box of fags sent out by some ole gal in 'Blighty,' an' when I got back to earth agen there weren't a bloomin' fag to be found. If thet ain't enough to mike a bloke swear, I dunno wot is. 'As any sport 'ere got a fag to gi' me? I ain't 'ad a smoke fer two days," he finished, "cept a li'l bit of a fag as the Keptin threw away."

Private Parkes hesitated for a minute, and then, seeing Joe Bates's eyes fixed expectantly on him, he produced a broken "Woodbine" from somewhere inside his cap.

"Yes," resumed "Pongo," while Joe Bates was lighting his cigarette, "this ain't what you'd call war. I wouldn't mind goin' for ole Fritz with an 'ammer, but, what with 'owitzers and 'crumps,' and 'Black Marias,' and 'pip-squeaks' and 'whizz-bangs,' the infantry bloke ain't got a chanst. 'Ere 'ave I been in a bloomin' trench for six months, and what 'ave I used my bay'nit for? To chop wood, and to wake ole Sandy when 'e snores. Down the line our blokes run over and give it to the Alleymans like 'ell, and up 'ere we sits jest like a lot of dolls while they send over those darned bombs. I'll give 'em what for. I'll put it acrost 'em." And he disappeared round the traverse with the canteen of tea for his officer.

Ten minutes later he turned up again with a jam tin bomb in his hand. "I bet I can reach their bloomin' listening post with this," he said, and he deliberately lit a piece of paper at the brazier fire and put it to the odd inch of fuse that protruded from the bomb. The average jam tin bomb is fused to burn for three or four seconds before it explodes, so that, once the fuse is lit, you do not keep the bomb near you for long, but send it across with your best wishes to Fritz over the way. "Pongo" drew his arm back to throw his bomb, and had begun the forward swing, when his fingers seemed to slip, and the weapon dropped down into the trench.

There was a terrific rush, and everyone disappeared helter-skelter round the traverse.

Just as Corporal Bateman rounded the corner into safety he glanced back, to see "Pongo" sprawling on his bomb in the most approved style, to prevent the bits from spreading. There was a long pause, during which the men crouched close to the parapet waiting, waiting ... but nothing happened.

At length someone poked his head round the traverse—to discover "Pongo" sitting on the sandbag recently vacated by Corporal Bateman, trying to balance the bomb on the point of a bayonet.

"'Ullo!" said that individual. "I thought as 'ow you'd gone 'ome for the week-end. 'E wouldn't 'urt me, not this little bloke," and he fondled the jam tin.

"Well," said Joe Bates when, one by one, the men had crept back to the fire, "if that ain't a bloomin' miracle! I ain't never seen nuffin' like it. Ain't you 'arf 'ad an escape, Pongo?"

"Pongo" rose to his feet, and edged towards the traverse. "It ain't such an escape as what you blokes think, because, you see, the bomb ain't nothin' more nor an ornary jam tin with a bit of fuse what I stuck in it."

And he disappeared down the trench as rapidly as had his comrades a few minutes before.

VI

THE SCHOOLMASTER OF PONT SAVERNE

I

"So, you see, Schoolmaster," said Oberleutnant von Scheldmann, "you French are a race of dogs. We are the real masters here, and, by Heaven, we have come to make you realise it. Your beloved defenders are running for their lives from the nation they ventured to defy a month ago. They are beaten, routed. What is it they say in your Latin books? 'Væ Victis.' Woe to the conquered!"

Gaston Baudel, schoolmaster in the little village of Pont Saverne, looked out of the window along the white road to Châlons-sur-Marne, four miles away. Between the poplar trees he could catch glimpses of it, and the river wound by its side, a broad ribbon of polished silver. From the road there rose, here and there, clouds of dust, telling of some battery or column on the move. The square of the little village, where he had lived for close on forty years, was crowded with German troops; the river was dirtied by hundreds of Germans, washing off the dust and blood; the inns echoed to German laughter and German songs, and, even as he looked, someone hurled a tray of glasses out of the window of the Lion d'Or into the street. His blood boiled with hate of the invading hosts that had so rudely aroused the sleepy, peaceful village, and he felt his self-control slipping, slipping....

"Get me some food," said the German suddenly. "We have hardly had one decent meal since your dogs of soldiers began running. Bring food and wine at once, so that I may go on and help to wipe the French and British scum from off the earth."

The insult was too much for Gaston Baudel. "May I be cursed," he shouted, "if I lift hand or foot to feed you and your like. I hate you all, for did you not kill my own father, when your soldiers overran France forty-four years ago! Go and find food elsewhere."

Von Scheldmann laughed to himself, amused at the Frenchman's rage. He leant out of the window, and called to his servant and another man, who were seated on the doorstep outside.

"Tie this fighting cock up with something," he ordered, "and go to see if there is anyone else in the house."

An unarmed schoolmaster is no even match for two armed and burly Germans. Gaston Baudel kicked and struggled as he had never done before, but he was old and weak, his eyes were watery through much reading, and his arm had none of the strength of youth left in it. In a few seconds he lay gasping on the floor, while a German, kneeling on him, tied his hands behind his back with strips of his own bedsheets.

"Now, you pig," said von Scheldmann when the soldiers had gone off to search the house, "remember that you are the conquered dog of a conquered race, and that my sword thirsts for French blood," and he added meaning to his words by drawing his weapon and pricking the schoolmaster's thin legs with it. "If I don't get food in a few minutes, I shall have to run this through your body."

Gaston Baudel had heard too much of war to put any trust in what we call "civilisation," which is, at best, merely a cloak that hides the savage beneath. He knew that the command to kill and pillage was more than enough to bring forth all the latent passions which man has tried to conceal since the days when he first clothed himself in skins; that it was no idle threat on the part of the German officer. He lay, then, in silence, on the floor of his own schoolroom, until the two soldiers returned, dragging between them the terrified Rosine, his old housekeeper.

"Are you the schoolmaster's servant?" asked von Scheldmann, in French.

Rosine nodded, for no words would come to her.

"Well, bring me the best food and wine in the house at once, or your master will suffer for it."

Rosine glanced at Gaston Baudel, who nodded to her as well as his position would allow him to. With tears in her eyes, the old servant hurried off to her kitchen to prepare the meal.

"Tie the schoolmaster down to that chair," ordered the German officer, "and place him opposite me, so that he may see how much his guest enjoys his lunch."

Thus they sat, the host and the guest, face to face across the little deal table near the window. The sun shone down on the clean cloth and the blood-coloured wine, and on the schoolmaster's grey hair. In the shade cast by the apple tree outside, sat the German, now drinking, now glancing mockingly at his unwilling host. The meal was interrupted by an orderly, who came in with a note.

Von Scheldmann read it, and swore. "In five minutes we parade," he said, "to follow on after your cowardly dogs of *poilus*. Here's a health to the new rulers of France! Here's to the German Empire!" and he leant across the table towards the schoolmaster. "Drink, you dog," he said, "drink to my toast," and he held his glass close to the other's lips.

Gaston Baudel hesitated for a moment. Then he suddenly jerked his head forward, and, with his chin, knocked the glass out of the German's hand. As the wine splashed over the floor, von Scheldmann leaped to his feet.

"Swine!" he shouted. "It is lucky for you that your wine was good and has left me in a kind mood, otherwise you would certainly die for that insult. As it is, you shall but lose your ears, and I shall benefit the world by cutting them off. If you move an inch I shall have to run my sword through your heart."

He lifted his sword, and brought it down twice. Then he called to his servant and hastened out into the sunlit street, leaving Gaston Baudel tied to his chair, with the warm blood running down each side of his face.

II

Six days later, shortly before the middle of September, an unwonted noise in the street brought the old schoolmaster from his breakfast. He walked down the little flagged path of the garden to the gate, and looked up and down the road. By the green, in the square, a group of villagers were talking and gesticulating, and from the direction of Ecury came the deep rumble of traffic and the sound of heavy firing.

The schoolmaster called to one of the peasants. "Hé, Jeanne," he cried. "What is the news?"

"The Boches are coming back, M. Baudel," said Jeanne Legrand. "They are fleeing from our troops, and will be passing through here, many of them. Pray God they may be in too much of a hurry to stop!" And her face grew anxious and frightened.

Old Gaston Baudel stepped out of his garden, and joined the group in the square. "Courage, mes amies," he said. "Even if they do stay awhile, even if our homes are shelled, what does it matter? France is winning, and driving the Germans back. That at any rate, is good news."

"All the same," said fat Madame Roland, landlady of the Lion d'Or, "if they break any more of my glasses, I shall want to break my last bottle of wine over their dirty heads." And she went off to hide what remained of her liqueurs and champagne under the sacking in the cellar.

"Let us all go back to our homes," counselled Gaston Baudel, "to hide anything of value. Even I, with this bandage round my head, can hear how swiftly they are retiring. There will, alas! be no school to-day. May our brave soldiers drive the devils from off our fair land of France."

Even as he spoke, the first transport waggons came tearing down the road, and swung northward over the river. Away in the morning haze, the infantry could be seen—dark masses stumbling along the white road—till a convoy of motor lorries hid them from view.

Gaston Baudel sat down in his stone-paved schoolroom to await the passing of the Germans, and to correct the tasks of his little pupils. He had given them a *devoir de style* to write on the glory of France, and, as he read the childish, ill-spelt prophecies of his country's greatness, he laughed, for the Germans were in retreat, the worst of the anxiety was over, and Paris was saved. And, hour by hour, he listened to the rumble of cannon, the rattle of transport waggons and ambulances, and the heavy tramp of tired-out soldiers on the dusty road.

Suddenly he heard the clank of boots coming up his little garden path, and a large figure loomed in the doorway. A German officer, covered with dirt, entered the room, and threw himself down in a chair.

"You still here, earless dog?" he said, and the schoolmaster recognised his tormentor of a week ago. "Give me something to take with me, and at once. I have no time to stop, but I shall certainly kill you this time if you don't bring me food, and more of that red wine."

Gaston Baudel glanced towards the drawer where he kept his revolver— though he would have never used it against any number of burglars—but a sudden idea came to him, and he checked his movement. With a few muttered words, he hastened off to the kitchen to get food for the German.

"Rosine," he said, "cut a sandwich for that German dog, and then run into my room and fetch the black sealing wax from my desk."

When she had gone off to obey him, Gaston Baudel opened a bottle of red wine and poured a little away. Then, fetching a small glass-stoppered bottle from his room, he emptied the contents—pure morphia—into the wine and recorked the bottle.

"So much," he said to himself, "for the doctor and his drugs. He may have told me how much to dilute it to deaden the pain of my ears, but he gave me no instructions about dosing Germans. They have strong stomachs; let them have strong drink."

But as he sealed the cork and mouth of the bottle, to allay any suspicions the German might have, a thought came to him. Was he not committing murder? Was he not taking away God's gift of life from a fellow creature? Unconsciously he touched the bandage that covered his mutilated ears. Surely, though, it could not be wrong to kill one of these hated oppressors? Should not an enemy of France be destroyed at any cost?

As he hesitated, the impatient voice of von Scheldmann sounded from the schoolroom. "You swine!" he shouted, "are you bringing me food, or must I come and fetch it?"

The schoolmaster seized a scrap of paper, and scribbled a few words on it. Then, slipping it between the cheese and bread of the sandwich, he made a little packet of the food, and hastened from the room. God, or Fate, must decide.

He handed the food and wine to the German, and watched him as he tramped down the garden path, to join in the unending stream of grey-coated soldiers who straggled towards the north.

III

Oberleutnant von Scheldmann sat on a bank by the roadside, to lunch in haste. Behind him, parallel to him, in front of him, went the German army; and the thunder of the guns, down by the Marne, told of the rearguard fight. As they tramped past, the soldiers gazed enviously at the bread and cheese and wine, for the country was clear of food, and, even had it not been, the rapid advance and rapid retreat left but little time for plundering.

Von Scheldmann knocked the top off the wine bottle with a blow from a stone, and, with care to avoid the sharp edges of the glass, he drank long and deep. As he bit greedily into the sandwich, his teeth met on something thin and tenuous, and he pulled the two bits of bread apart. Inside was a scrap of paper. With a curse, he was about to throw the paper away, when some pencilled words caught his eye.

"I leave it to God," he read, "to decide whether you live or die. If you have not drunk any wine, do not, for it is poisoned. If you have, you are lost, and nothing can save you. The victorious French will find your corpse, and will rejoice. Væ victis! Woe to the conquered!"

And even as he read the hurriedly written words, von Scheldmann felt the first awful sense of numbness that presaged the end.

VII

THE ODD JOBS

We sat in a railway carriage and told each other, as civilians love to do, what was the quickest way to end the war. "You ought to be able to hold nearly 400 yards of trench with a company," my friend was saying. "You see, a company nowadays gives you 250 fighting men to man the trenches."

And then the muddy figure in the corner, the only other occupant of the carriage, woke up. "You don't know what you're talking about," he snorted as he tossed his cap up on to the rack, and put his feet on the opposite seat.

"You don't know what you're talking about," he repeated. "You're lucky if your company can produce more than 150 men to man the trenches; you forget altogether about the odd jobs. Take the company I'm in at the front, for instance. Do you imagine we've got 250 men to man the trenches? First of all there are always men being hit and going sick, or men who are sent off to guard lines of communication, and their places aren't filled up by fresh drafts for weeks. As for the odd jobs, there's no end to them. My own particular pal is a telephone orderly—he sits all day in a dug-out and wakes up at stated hours to telephone 'No change in the situation' to battalion headquarters. It's true that he does jolly good work when the Huns 'strafe' his wire and he has to go out and mend it, but he doesn't go forward in an attack; he sits in his dug-out and telephones like blazes for reinforcements while the Germans pepper his roof for him with 'whizz-bangs.'

"Then there's old Joe White, the man like a walrus, who left us months ago to go and guard divisional headquarters; there are five officers' servants who are far too busy to man a trench; there is a post corporal, who goes down to meet the transport every night to fetch the company's letters, and who generally brings up a sack of bread by mistake or drops the parcels into shell holes that are full of water; there's a black, greasy fellow who calls himself a cook, and who looks after a big 'tank' called a 'cooker,' from which he extracts oily tea, and meat covered with tea-leaves. Besides all these fellows there are sixteen sanitary men who wander about with tins of chloride of lime and keep the trench clean—they don't man the trenches; then there are three battalion orderlies, who run about with messages from headquarters and who wake the captain up, as soon as he gets to sleep, to ask him to state in writing how much cheese was issued to his men yesterday or why Private X has not had his hair cut.

"Do you imagine this finishes the list? Not a bit of it. There are half a dozen machine gunners who have nothing to do with company work; half a dozen men and a quartermaster-sergeant attached to the transport to look after the horses and to flirt with girls in farms; two mess waiters whose job it is to feed the officers; and there are four men who have the rottenest time of anyone—they're the miners who burrow and dig, dig and burrow day and night towards the German lines; poor half-naked fellows who wheel little trucks of earth to the pit shaft or who lie on their stomachs working away with picks. And it's always an awful race to see if they'll blow up the Germans, or if it will be the other way about.

"There are still more odd jobs, and new ones turn up every day. Mind you, I'm not grumbling, for many of these fellows work harder than we do, and we must have someone to feed us and to keep the place clean. But the difficulty is nowadays to find a man who's got time to stand in the trench and wait for the Hun to attack, and that's what you people don't seem to realise."

"And what do you do?" asked my friend as the other stopped to yawn.

"What do I do? What do you think I've been talking for all this time?" said the man in khaki. "I'm the fellow who stands in the trench and waits for the Hun to attack. That's a jolly long job, and I've got some sleep owing to me for it, too."

Whereupon he stretched himself out on the seat, pillowed his head on his pack, and proceeded to extract noisy payment of his debt.

"That rather complicates matters, doesn't it?" said my friend, when the muddy figure had safely reached the land of dreams. "If you've only got 150 fighting men in a company, your division has a strength of ..." and he proceeded to count away on his fingers as hard as he could. Presently he gave it up in despair, and a brilliant idea seemed to strike him.

"Those generals and staff fellows," he said, "must have a lot of brains after all." And we have come to the conclusion that we will not criticise them any more, for they must know as well as we do, if not still better, how to win the war.

VIII

THE "KNUT"

We were sitting round the fire in the club, discussing that individual colloquially known as the "knut."

"The 'knut,'" said Green, "is now virtually extinct, he is killed by war. As soon as he gets anywhere near a trench, he drops his cloak of affectation, and becomes a reasonable human being—always excepting, of course, certain young subalterns on the staff."

Rawlinson leant forward in his chair. "I'm not sure," he said, "that I agree with you. It all depends upon how you define a 'knut.'"

"A 'knut' is a fellow with a drawl and an eyeglass," said someone.

"That just fits my man. I know of an exception to your rule. I know of a 'knut' who did not disappear at the front."

"Tell us about him," suggested Jepson.

Rawlinson hesitated, and glanced round at each of us in turn. "It's not much of a story," he said at length, "but it stirred me up a bit at the time—I don't mind telling it you if you think it sufficiently interesting."

We filled up our glasses, and lay back in our chairs to listen to the following tale:

"When I was at Trinity I kept rooms just above a fellow called Jimmy Wynter. He wasn't a pal of mine at all, as he had far too much money to chuck about—one of these rich young wastrels, he was. He could drop more than my annual allowance on one horse, and not seem to notice it at all. In the end he got sent down for some rotten affair, and I was rather glad to see the last of him, as the row from his rooms was appalling. He always had an eyeglass and wonderfully cut clothes, and his hair was brushed back till it was as shiny as a billiard ball. I put him down, as did everyone else, as an out-and-out rotter, and held him up as an example of our decadent aristocracy.

"When I went out to the front, our Regular battalion was full up, and I was sent to a Welsh regiment instead. The first man I met there was none other than this fellow Wynter, still with his eyeglass and his drawl. In time, one got quite accustomed to him, and he was always fairly amusing—which, of course, is a great thing out there—so that in the end I began to like him in a sort of way.

"All this seems rot, but it helps to give you an idea of my man, and it all leads up to my story, such as it is.

"We came in for that Loos show last year. After months and months of stagnation in the trenches, we were suddenly called to Headquarters and told that we were to make an attack in about two hours' time.

"I don't know if any of you fellows came in for a bayonet charge when you were out at the Front. Frankly, I felt in a hell of a funk, for it's not the same thing to leave your trench and charge as it is to rush an enemy after you've been lying in an open field for an hour or two. The first hour and a half went all right, what with fusing bombs, arranging signals, and all that sort of thing, but the last half-hour was the very devil.

"Most of us felt a bit jumpy, and the double rum ration went in two shakes. We knew that we shouldn't worry when the whistles went for the charge, but the waiting was rather trying. Personally I drank more neat brandy than I have ever done before or since, and then sat down and tried to write one or two letters. But it wasn't a brilliant success, and I soon left my dug-out and strolled along to C Company.

"The idea was for A and C Companies to attack first, followed by B and D companies. A battalion of the Westshires was in support to us.

"C Company Officer's dug-out was not a mental haven of rest. With one exception, everyone was a bit nervy, everyone was trying not to show it, and everyone was failing dismally. The exception was Jimmy Wynter. He was sitting on a pile of sandbags in the corner, his eyeglass in his eye, looking at an old copy of *La Vie Parisienne*, with evident relish. His hand was as steady as a rock, and he hadn't had a drop of rum or brandy to give him Dutch courage. While everyone else was fighting with excitement, Jimmy Wynter was sitting there, studying the jokes of his paper, as calmly as though he were sitting here in this old club. It was only then that it occurred to me that there was something in the fellow after all.

"At last the time drew near for our push, and we waited, crouching under the parapet, listening to our artillery plunking away like blazes. At last the whistles blew, a lot of fellows cheered, yelled all sorts of idiotic things, and A and C Companies were over the parapet on the way to the Huns.

"I am no hand at a description of a charge, but it really was wonderful to watch those fellows; the sight of them sent every vestige of funk from me, and the men could hardly wait for their turn to come. Just before we went, I had one clear vision of Jimmy Wynter. He was well ahead of his platoon, for he was over six foot and long-legged at that. I could see his eyeglass swinging on the end of its black cord, and in his hand he carried a pickaxe. Such ordinary weapons as revolvers, rifles, and bayonets had no apparent attraction for him.

"What happened next I had no time to see, for our turn came to hop over the parapet, and there wasn't much time to think of other people. Allan, his servant, told me later all that occurred, for he was next to Jimmy all the time. They got to the Hun trenches and lost a lot of men on the wire. Away to the left the enemy had concealed a crowd of machine guns in one of the slag heaps, and they played awful havoc among our chaps. According to Allan, Jimmy chose a place where the wire had almost all gone, took a huge leap over the few remaining strands, and was the first of C Company to get into the trench.

"Somehow he didn't get touched—I'll bet Allan had something to do with that; for he loved his master. With his pick he cracked the skull of the first Boche who showed signs of fight, and, losing his hold of his weapon, he seized the man's rifle as he fell. No wonder the poor blighters fled, for Jimmy Wynter must have looked like Beelzebub as he charged down on them. His hat had gone, and his hair stuck out from his head like some modern Struwwelpeter. With the rifle swinging above his head, he did as much to clear the trench as did the rest of the platoon all put together.

"When we arrived on the scene the few who remained of A and C Companies were well on their way to the second line of trenches. Here again Jimmy Wynter behaved like a demon with his rifle and bayonet, and in five minutes' time we were in complete possession of two lines of trenches along a front of two hundred yards. I do not even mention the number of Germans that Allan swore his master had disposed of, but the name of Wynter will long be a by-word in the regiment. The funny part of it is that, up to that time, he hadn't had a single scratch. However, Fate may overlook a man for a short time, but he is generally remembered in the end. So it was with poor old Jimmy.

"He was leading a party down a communicating trench, bombing the Huns back yard by yard, when a hand grenade landed almost at his feet. He jumped forward, in the hope that he would have time to throw it away before it went off, but it was fused too well. Just as he picked it up, the damned thing exploded, and Jimmy Wynter crumpled up like a piece of paper.

"I was coming along the trench a few minutes later, seeing that our position was being made as secure as possible before the counter-attack came, when I found him. He was lying in one of the few dug-outs that had not been hit, and Allan and another man were doing what they could for him.

"You could see he was very nearly done for, but, after a few seconds, he opened his eyes and recognised me.

"'Hullo, Rawlinson,' he whispered; 'some damned fool has hit me. Hurts like the very devil.'

"I muttered some banal words of comfort, and continued to tie him up—though God knows it was a pretty hopeless task. I hadn't even any morphia I could give him to make things better.

"Suddenly he raised his arm and fumbled about in search of something.

"'What do you want?' I asked.

"'Where the deuce is my eyeglass?' And the drawl seemed to catch horribly in his throat.

"I put the rim of the eyeglass into his hand; the glass itself had gone.

"'Must wear the damned thing,' he murmured, and he tried to raise it to his face—but his hand suddenly stopped half-way and fell, and he died."

There was silence in the club room for a minute or so, and the ticking of the clock was oppressively loud. Then Jepson raised his glass.

"Gentlemen," he said. "Here's to the 'Knut,'" and gravely we drank to the toast.

IX

SHOPPING

As the Captain sat down to breakfast, he turned to speak to me: "I propose ..." he began, but Lawson interrupted him. "Oh, John dear," he said, "this is so sudden."

The Captain took no notice of the interruption. "... that you and I go shopping this afternoon."

"Jane," I called to an imaginary maid, "please tell Parkes to bring the car round at eleven o'clock; we are going shopping in Bond Street, and lunching at the Ritz."

"You all seem to think you're deucedly funny this morning," growled the Captain as he pushed aside a piece of cold bacon with the end of his knife. "The pure air of the billets seems to have gone to your heads so that I think a parade would suit you this afternoon."

We sobered down at the threat. "No, seriously," I said, "I'd love to go if I can get anything to ride."

"You can have the Company's pack horse. I'll order both beasts for two o'clock."

Now the Captain's horse stands far more hands than any really respectable horse should, and the Captain is well over six feet in his socks; I, on the other hand, am nearer five feet than six, and the pack pony is none too big for me. Again, the Captain is thin and I am fat, so that even the sentry could scarcely repress his smile as we set forth on our quest—a modern Don Quixote, and a Sancho Panza with a hole in the back of his tunic.

But we had little time to think of our personal appearances, for our way lay over the Mont Noir, and there are few places from which you can get a more wonderful view, for you can follow the firing line right away towards the sea, and your field glasses will show you the smoke rising from the steamers off Dunkirk. We paused a moment, and gazed over the level miles where Poperinghe and Dixmude and the distant Furnes lay sleepy and peaceful, but, even as we looked, a "heavy" burst in Ypres, and a long column of smoke rose languidly from the centre of the town.

"We shan't do much more shopping in that old spot," said the Captain as he turned his horse off the road, and set forth across country to Bailleul.

The Captain has hunted with nearly every pack of hounds in England, while I have hunted with none, so that I was hot and thirsty and uncommonly sore when we clattered into the town. Leaving the Captain to see the horses stabled at the Hôtel du Faucon, I slipped off to get a drink.

"Here," said the Captain when he tracked me down, "don't try that game on again or you'll have to take the early parade to-morrow. Besides, you're supposed to be Company Interpreter, and you've no right to leave me to the mercy of two savage grooms like that. I advise you to take care, young man."

My qualifications for the post of Company Interpreter lie in the fact that I once, in company of various other youths of my age, spent a fortnight in and around the Casino at Trouville. Peters of our company knows a long list of nouns taking "x" instead of "s" in the plural, but my knowledge is considered more practical—more French.

And now comes a confession. To retain a reputation requires a lot of care, and to keep my position as Company Interpreter and outdo my rival Peters I always carried about with me a small pocket dictionary—if anyone ever noticed it, he probably mistook it for a Service Bible—in which I searched for words when occasion offered. I had carefully committed to memory the French equivalents for all the articles on our shopping list—a pot of honey, a bottle of Benedictine, a pair of unmentionable garments for Lawson, and a toothbrush—so that I walked across the main square with a proud mien and an easy conscience.

Pride, they tell us, comes before a fall. We had successfully fought our way through the crowds of officers and mess waiters who swarm in Bailleul, we had completed our purchases, we were refreshing ourselves in a diminutive tea shop, when the Captain suddenly slapped his thigh.

"By Jove," he said, "I promised to buy a new saucepan for the Company cook. Good job I remembered."

What on earth was the French for a saucepan? I had no opportunity of looking in my dictionary, for it would look too suspicious if I were to consult my Service Bible during tea.

"I don't think we shall have time to look for an ironmonger's," I said.

"You blithering ass," said the Captain, "there's one just across the road. Besides, we don't have dinner before eight as a rule."

The fates were working against me. I made one more effort to save my reputation. "We should look so funny, sir, riding through Bailleul with a great saucepan. We might send the Company cook to buy one to-morrow."

I remained in suspense for a few moments as the Captain chose another cake. He looked up suddenly. "We'll get it home all right," he said, "but I believe the fact of the matter is that you don't know what to ask for."

"We'll go and get the beastly thing directly after tea," I said stiffly, for it is always offensive to have doubts cast on one's capabilities, the more so when those doubts are founded on fact. Besides, I knew the Captain would love to see me at a loss, as French has been his touchy point ever since the day when, having a sore throat, he set out to buy a cure for it himself. The chemist, mistaking his French and his gestures, had politely led him to the door and pointed out a clothier's across the way, expressing his regret the while that chemists in France do not sell collars.

When we entered the ironmonger's shop I could see nothing in the shape of a saucepan that I could point out to the man, so I made a shot in the dark. "Je désire," I said, "une soucoupe."

"Parfaitement, m'sieu," said the shopman, and he produced a host of saucers of every description—saucers in tin, saucers in china, saucers big and little.

"What in the name of all that's wonderful are you getting those things for?" asked the Captain irritably. "We want a saucepan."

I feigned surprise at my carelessness and turned to the shopman again. "Non, je désire quelque chose pour bouillir les œufs."

The poor man scratched his head for a minute, then an idea suddenly struck him. "Ah, une casserole?" he questioned.

I nodded encouragingly, and, to my intense relief, he produced a huge saucepan from under the counter, so that we trotted out of Bailleul with our saddle bags full, and the saucepan dangling from a piece of string round the Captain's neck.

Misfortunes never come singly. We were not more than a hundred yards from the town when the Captain handed the saucepan to me. "You might take it," he said, "while I shorten my stirrups."

The pack horse becomes accustomed to an enormous variety of loads, but apparently the saucepan was something in the shape of a disagreeable novelty to him. He began to trot, and that utensil rattled noisily against the bottle of liqueur protruding from my saddle bag. The more the saucepan rattled the faster went the horse, and the more precarious became my seat. In a few seconds I was going across country at a furious gallop.

If I let go my hold of the saucepan it rattled violently, and spurred the pack horse on to even greater pace; if I held on to the saucepan I could not pull up my horse and I stood but little chance of remaining on its back at all, for I am a horseman of but very little skill.

Suddenly I saw a gate barring my way ahead. I let go the saucepan and something cracked in my saddle bag. I seized the reins and dragged at the horse's mouth. Then, just as I was wondering how one stuck on a horse's back when it tried to jump, someone rode up from the other side and opened the gate.

But it was only when I was right in the gateway that I saw what lay ahead. Just before me was a major at the head of a squadron of cavalry. The next second I was amongst them.

A fleeting glimpse of the Major's horse pawing the air with its forelegs, a scattering of a hundred and fifty men before me, and I had passed them all and was galloping up the steep slope of the hill.

When at last the Captain came up with me, I was standing at the top of the Mont Noir, wiping Benedictine from my breeches and puttees. I made an attempt at jocularity. "I shall have to speak to Parkes about this engine," I said. "The controls don't work properly, and she accelerates much too quickly."

But the Captain saw the ruin of the liqueur bottle lying by the roadside, and was not in the mood for amusement. So we rode in silence down the hill, while the flames of Ypres gleamed and flickered in the distance.

Of a sudden, however, the Captain burst into a roar of laughter.

"It was worth it," he panted as he rolled in his saddle, "to see the poor blighters scatter. Lord! but it was lovely to hear that Major curse."

X

THE LIAR

For an hour and a half we had been crumped and whizz-banged and trench-mortared as never before, but it was not until the shelling slackened that one could really see the damage done. The sudden explosions of whizz-bangs, the increasing whine and fearful bursts of crumps, and, worst of all, the black trench-mortar bombs that came hurtling and twisting down from the skies, kept the nerves at a pitch which allowed of no clear vision of the smashed trench and the wounded men.

However, as the intervals between the explosions grew longer and longer the men gradually pulled themselves together and began to look round. The havoc was appalling. Where the telephone dug-out had been was now a huge hole—a mortar bomb had landed there, and had blown the telephone orderly almost on to the German wire, fifty yards away; great gaps, on which the German machine guns played at intervals, were made all along our parapet; the casualties were being sorted out as well as possible—the dead to be carried into an old support trench, and there to await burial, the wounded to be hurried down to the overcrowded dressing station as quickly as the bearers could get the stretchers away; the unhurt—scarcely half the company—were, for the most part, still gazing up into the sky in the expectation of that twisting, all too familiar, black bomb that has such a terrific devastating power. Gradually quiet came again, and the men set about their interrupted business—their sleep to be snatched, their work to be finished before the long night with its monotonous watching and digging began.

With the Sergeant-major I went down the trench to discuss repairs, for much must be done as soon as night fell. Then, leaving him to make out a complete list of the casualties, I returned to my dug-out to share the rations of rum with Bennett, the only subaltern who remained in the company.

"Where's the rum?" I asked. "Being shelled makes one thirsty."

He handed me a cup, at the bottom of which a very little rum was to be seen. "I divided it as well as I could," he said rather apologetically.

"If you were thinking of yourself at the time, you certainly did," I answered as I prepared myself for battle, for nothing sets your nerves right again as quickly as a "scrap."

We were interrupted, however, in the preliminaries by the Sergeant-major, who brought with him a handful of letters and pay books, the effects of the poor fellows who were now lying under waterproof sheets in the support trench.

"Total killed forty-one, sir, and I'm afraid Sergeant Wall didn't get down to the dressing station in time. It's a bad day for us to-day. Oh, and by the way, sir, that fellow Spiller has just been found dead at the end of the communicating trench."

"Which end, Sergeant-major?" I asked.

"The further end, sir. He left the trench without leave. He told Jones, who was next to him, that he was not going to have any more damned shelling, and he appears to have made off immediately after."

Bennett whistled. "Is that the blighter whom poor old Hayes had to threaten with his revolver the day before we were gassed?"

The Sergeant-major nodded.

"It's just the sort of thing he would do," said Bennett, whose hand was still unsteady from the strain of an hour ago, "to bunk when Brother Boche is giving us a little crumping to keep us amused."

I turned to the Sergeant-major. "Let me have these fellows' effects," I said. "As to Spiller, I don't expect he could have really been bunking. At all events, let the other fellows think I sent him to Headquarters and he got hit on the way. I expect he was going down with a stretcher party." But, in my heart, I knew better. I knew Spiller for a coward.

It is not for me to judge such a man. God knows it is no man's fault if he is made so that his nerves may fail him at a critical moment. Besides, many a man who is capable of heroism that would win him the Victoria Cross fails when called upon to stand more than a few weeks of trench warfare, for a few minutes of heroism are very different to months of unrelieved strain. However, Spiller and his like let a regiment down, and one is bound to despise them for that.

Thoughts of our "scrap" had entirely left us, for Bennett and I had before us one of the most uncongenial tasks that an officer can have. The news has to be broken by someone when a wife is suddenly made a widow, and the task is generally taken on by the dead man's platoon commander, who sends back home his letters and papers. There were many men who had died that afternoon, and letters of condolence and bad news are always difficult to write, so that there was silence in our dug-out for the next two hours.

The last pay book I examined had belonged to Private E. Spiller. His other belongings were scanty—a few coppers, a much-chewed pencil, and two letters. I looked at the latter for a clue as to whom I ought to write; one was in his own handwriting and unfinished, the other was from a girl with whom he had been "walking out," apparently his only friend in the world, as she alone was mentioned in the little will written at the end of his pay book. But her love was enough. Her letter was ill-spelt and badly written, but it expressed more love than is given to most men.

"Take care of yourself, Erny dear, for my sake," she wrote. "I am so proud of you doing so well in them horrid trenches.... Dear Erny, you can't have no idear how pleased I am that you are so brave, but be quick and come back to me what loves you so...."

So brave! I tried to laugh at the unconscious irony of it all, but my laugh would not come, for something in my throat held it back—perhaps I was a little overwrought by the recent shelling.

I turned to the other letter, which I have thought fit to transcribe in full:

"DEAREST LIZ,

"I hope this finds you as it leaves me at present in the pink. Dear Liz, i am doing very well and i will tell you a secret—i am going to be rekermended for the V.C. becos i done so well in the trenches. i don't feel a bit fritened wich is nice, and, dear Liz, i hope to be made Lance Corpril soon as my officer is so ..."

And here it ended, this letter from a liar. I balanced it on my knee and wondered what to do with it. Should I tear it up and write to the girl to tell her the truth—that her lover was a liar and a coward? Should I tear his letter up and just announce his death? For some minutes I hesitated, and then I put his half-finished letter in an envelope and added a note to tell her.

"He died like a soldier," I finished. "His letter will tell you better than any words of mine how utterly without fear he was."

And I wish no other lie were heavier on my conscience than is the lie I told to her.

XI

THE CITY OF TRAGEDY

What does it matter that the Cloth Hall and the Cathedral are in ruins, that the homes and churches are but rubble in the streets? What do we care if great shells have torn gaping holes in the Grande Place, and if the station is a battered wreck where the rails are bent and twisted as bits of wire? We do not mourn for Ypres, for it is a thousand times grander in its downfall than it was ever in the days of its splendour.

In the town, the houses are but piles of stone, the streets are but pitted stretches of desolation, the whole place is one huge monument to the memory of those who have suffered, simply and grandly, for a great cause. Round the town run the green ramparts where, a few years ago, the townspeople would stroll of an evening, where the blonde Flemish girls would glance shyly and covertly at the menfolk. The ramparts now are torn, the poplars are broken, the moat is foul and sullied, and facing out over the wide plain are rows of little crosses that mark the resting-places of the dead.

For herein lies thy glory, Ypres. To capture thee there have fallen thousands of the German invaders; in thy defence there have died Belgians and French and English, Canadians and Indians and Algerians. Three miles away, on Hill 60, are the bodies of hundreds of men who have fought for thee—the Cockney buried close to the Scotchman, the Prussian lying within a yard of the Prussian who fell there a year before, and along the Cutting are French bayonets and rifles, and an occasional unfinished letter from some long-dead *poilu* to his lover in the sunny plains of the Midi or the orchards of Normandy.

And all these men have died to save thee, Ypres. Why, then, should we mourn for thee in thy ruin? Even thy great sister, Verdun, cannot boast so proud a record as thine.

But the awful tragedy of it all! That the famous old town, quietly asleep in its plain, should be shattered and ruined; that so many hopes and ambitions can be blasted in so few hours; that young bodies can be crushed, in a fraction of a second, to masses of lifeless, bleeding pulp! The glorious tragedy of Ypres will never be written, for so many who could have spoken are dead, and so many who live will never speak—you can but guess their stories from the dull pain in their eyes, and from the lips that they close tightly to stop the sobs.

God, how they have suffered, these Belgians! Day after day for over a year the inhabitants of Ypres lived in the hell of war; day after day they crouched in their cellars and wondered if it would be their little home that would be ruined by the next shell. How many lived for months in poky little basements, or crowded together in the one room that was left of their home—anything, even death, rather than leave the place where they were born and where they had passed all their quiet, happy years.

I knew one woman who lived with her little daughter near the Porte de Menin, and one day, when the next cottage to hers had been blown to bits, I tried to persuade her to leave. For a long time she shook her head, and then she took me to show me her bedroom—such a poor little bedroom, with a crucifix hanging over the bed and a dingy rosebush growing up outside the window. "It was here that my husband died, five years ago," she said. "He would not like me to go away and leave the house to strangers."

"But think of the little one," I pleaded. "She is only a girl of five, and you cannot endanger her life like this."

For a long time she was silent, and a tear crept down her cheek as she tried to decide. "I will go, monsieur," she said at last, "for the sake of the little one."

And that night she set off into the unknown, fearful to look back at her little home lest her courage should desert her. She was dressed in her best clothes—for why leave anything of value for the Germans, should they ever come?—and she wheeled her few household treasures before her in the perambulator, while her little daughter ran beside her.

But next morning I saw her again coming back up the street to her cottage. This time she was alone, and she still trundled the perambulator in front of her.

I went out, and knocked at her door. "So you have come back," I said. "And where have you left the little one?"

She gazed at me dully for a minute, and a great fear gripped me, for I saw that her best clothes were torn and dust stained.

"It was near the big hospital on the Poperinghe road," she said in a horribly even voice. "The little one had lingered behind to pick up some bits of coloured glass on the roadside when the shell came. It was a big shell ... and I could find nothing but this," and she held up part of a little torn dress, bloody and terrible.

I tried to utter a few words of comfort, but my horror was too great.

"It is the will of God," she said, as she began to unpack the treasures in the perambulator, but, as I closed the door, I heard her burst into the most awful fit of weeping I have ever known.

And, day by day as the war goes on, the tragedy of Ypres grows greater. Each shell wrecks a little more of what was once a home, each crash and falling of bricks brings a little more pain to a breaking heart. The ruins of Ypres are glorious and noble, and we are proud to defend them, but the quiet, simple people of Ypres cannot even find one brick on another of their homes.

Somewhere in England, they tell me, is a little old lady who was once a great figure in Brussels society. She is nearly eighty now, and alone, but she clings on tenaciously to life till the day shall come when she can go back to her Château at Ypres, where she has lived for forty years. One can picture her—feeble, wizened, and small, her eyes bright with the determination to live until she has seen her home again.

I, who have seen her Château, pray that death may come to close those bright eyes, so that they may never look upon the destruction of her home, for it is a desolate sight, even though the sky was blue and the leaves glistened in the sun on the morning when, two years ago, I tramped up the winding drive.

The lodge was nothing more than a tumbled pile of broken bricks, but, by some odd chance, the Château itself had never suffered a direct hit. In front of the big white house there had once been an asphalt tennis court—there was now a plain pitted at every few yards by huge shell holes. The summer-house at the edge of the wood—once the scene of delightful little flirtations in between the games of tennis—was now a weird wreck, consisting of three tottering walls and a broken seat. Oddest of all, there lay near the white marble steps an old, tyreless De Dion motor-car.

I have often wondered what the history of that battered thing could be. One can almost see the owner packing herself in it with her most precious belongings, to flee from the oncoming Germans. The engine refuses to start, there is no time for repairs, there is the hurried flight on foot, and the car is left to the mercy of the invading troops. Perhaps, again, it belonged to the staff of some army, and was left at the Château when it had run its last possible mile. At all events, there it stood, half-way between Ypres and the Germans, with everything of any possible value stripped off it as thoroughly as though it had been left to the white ants.

By the side of the tennis court, where had once been flower beds, there was now a row of little, rough wooden crosses, and here and there the narcissi and daffodils had sprung up. What a strange little cemetery! Here a khaki cap and a bunch of dead flowers, there a cross erected to "An unknown British hero, found near Verbrandenmolen and buried here on March 3rd, 1915," there an empty shell case balanced at a comical angle on a grave, and everywhere between the mounds waved the flowers in the fresh breeze of the morning, while away in the distance loomed the tower of the Cloth Hall of Ypres, like a gigantic arm pointing one finger up to heaven.

The Château itself, I have said, had never had a direct hit; but do you think the hand of war had passed it by, and that the little old lady would find in it something of home?

Every window on the ground floor had been choked by sandbags, and no glass remained in those upstairs. In a room that had once been a kitchen and was now labelled in chalk "Officers' Mess" were an old bedstead, two mattresses, a wooden table, and three rickety chairs; but for these, and a piano in the dining-room upstairs, the house was absolutely devoid of furniture. Even the piano, which must have twanged out the tunes of at least three nations since the war began, had sacrificed its cover for firewood.

Rooms where once ladies had powdered and perfumed themselves to attract the fickle male were now bare and empty, and pungent with the smell of chloride of lime. In the dining-hall, where fine old wines had circulated, were a hundred weary, dirty men. In the kitchen, where the fat *cuisinière* had prepared her dinners, were now a dozen officers, some sprawling asleep on the floor, some squatting round the table playing "vingt-et-un."

For this is war.

There is one more memory of Ypres—a very different one—that comes back to me. It is the recollection of our regimental dinner.

The first thing that I heard of it came from Lytton's servant.

"Please, sir," he said one morning, "Mr. Lytton sends his compliments, and can you tell 'im where the Hôtel Delepiroyle is?"

"The Hôtel de what?"

"The Hôtel Delepiroyle, sir. That's what 'e said."

"Ask Mr. Lytton to write it down—no, wait a minute. Tell him I'm coming over to see him about it." So I strolled across to the other side of the infantry barracks to find him.

"What, haven't you heard about it?" asked Lytton. "The new C.O., Major Eadie, is giving a dinner to-night to all the officers of the regiment as a farewell to Major Barton before he goes off to take command of his new crowd. It's at the Hôtel de l'Epée Royale, wherever that may be. Let's go and track it down."

So we wandered down the Rue de Lille, as yet relatively free from the ravages of war, for the shops were open and the inhabitants stood talking and gossiping at the doors of their houses. Here and there rubble lay across the pavement, and what had once been a home was now an amorphous pile of bricks and beams. Just by the church was a ruined restaurant, and a host of little children played hide and seek behind the remnants of its walls.

On our way down the street we came across Reynolds, who had only joined the regiment the night before, while we, who had been nearly three weeks at the front, felt ourselves war-beaten veterans compared to him. He was standing on the pavement, gazing excitedly up at an aeroplane, around which were bursting little white puffs of smoke.

"Come along with us," said Lytton. "You'll get sick to death of seeing aeroplanes shelled when you've been out here as long as we have. Come and discover the scene of to-night's orgy."

In the Grande Place, at the side of the Cloth Hall, we discovered the Hôtel de l'Epée Royale. A "Jack Johnson" had made an enormous hole in the pavement just in front of it, and a large corner of the building had gone.

"By Jove," said Reynolds in an awed voice. "What a hole! It must have taken some shell to do that."

Lytton smiled patronisingly. "My dear fellow," he said, "that's nothing at all. It's hardly any bigger than the hole that a spent bullet makes. Let's go inside and get some lunch to see what sort of a place it is."

But Reynolds and I were firm. "Rot!" we said. "Let's go home and fast. Otherwise we shall be no good for this evening; we've got our duty to do to the dinner."

So we went back to the Company Mess in the infantry barracks, past a house that had been destroyed that morning. Hunting in and out of the ruins were a man and a woman, and another woman, very old, with eyes swollen by weeping, sat on what was left of the wall of her house, a broken photograph frame in her hands.

There are many fellows who have laid down their lives since that little dinner in the Hôtel de l'Epée Royale; he who gave it died of wounds six weeks later, as gallant a commanding officer as one could wish to have. If the dinner were to take place again, there would be many gaps round the table, and even the building must long since have been pounded to dust.

If this should meet the eyes of any of you that were there, let your minds run back for a moment, and smile at your recollections. Do you remember how we dosed Wilson's glass so that he left us before the sweets were on the table? Do you remember how we found him later sitting on the stairs, poor fellow, clasping his head in a vain effort to stop the world from whirling round? Do you remember the toasts that we drank, and the plans we made for that dim period, "after the war"? I confess that I have completely forgotten everything that we ate—beyond the whisky, I forget even what we drank; but I know that the daintiest little dinner in London could not have pleased us nearly so much. And then, when it was all over and we broke up to go home to bed, do you remember how young Carter stood in the middle of the Grande Place and made rhapsodies to the moon—though, to the rest of us, it seemed much like any other moon—until we took him up and carried him home by force?

It does you good to look back sometimes. You may find it sad because so many are gone that were our companions then. But this is the way of war; they must die sooner or later, and they could not have chosen better graves. If one must die, why not die fighting for England and Ypres?

There is one street in Ypres that I knew in peace time. It wound in and out between the stiff, white houses, and the little Flemish children would make it echo to their shouts and laughter, until you could scarcely hear the rumble and the rattle of the carts on the cobbles of the main street, near by. And I passed along the same winding way during the second battle of Ypres. The shattered houses stretched jagged edges of brickwork towards the sky, the road was torn up, and the paving stones were piled up grotesquely against each other. Outside the convent, where I seemed to catch the dim echo of children's laughter, lay a smashed limber—the horse was on its back, with its legs stuck up stiffly; and, just touching the broken stone cross that had fallen from above the convent door, lay the figure of the dead driver.

And, of all that I remember of Ypres, it is of this that I think most often, for it is a symbol of the place itself—the dead man lying by the cross, sign of suffering that leads to another life. The agony of Ypres will render it immortal; for if ever a town deserved immortality, it is surely this old, ruined city on the plains of Flanders.

XII

"PONGO" SIMPSON ON GRUMBLERS

I was in my dug-out, trying to write a letter by the intermittent light of a candle which was extinguished from time to time by the rain drops that came through the roof, when I suddenly heard the squelching of mud, the sound of slipping, and an appalling splash. Someone had fallen into the shell hole just outside.

I waited a moment, and I heard the well-known voice of "Pongo" Simpson. "Strike me pink!" he spluttered, as he scrambled up the steep bank out of the water. "An' I gone an' forgot me soap. The first bath as I've 'ad for six weeks, too." And he blundered into my dug-out, a terrible object covered in slimy mud from head to foot, and when he breathed little showers of mud flew off his moustache.

"Hullo," I said, "you seem to be wet."

"Sorry, sir," said "Pongo," "I thought as 'ow this was my dug-out. Wet, sir? Gawd! Yes, I should think I was wet," and he doubled up to show me, while a thin stream of muddy water trickled from his hair on to my letter. "'Owever, it ain't no good to grumble, an' it's better to fall in a shell hole than to 'ave a shell fall on me. I've got some 'ot tea in me own dug-out, too."

When he had gone, I crumpled up my muddy letter, and I confess that I purposely listened to his conversation, for his dug-out was only separated from mine by a few horizontal logs piled up on each other.

"Well, you see, it ain't no good to grouse," he was saying to someone. "I've got mud up me nose an' in me eyes, and all down me neck, but it won't go away 'owever much I grumbles. Now, there's some blokes as grouses all the time—'ere, Bert, you might 'and over your knife a moment to scrape the mud off me face, it all cracks, like, when I talk—if they've got a Maconochie ration they wants bully beef, an' if they've got bully beef they carn't abear nothink but Maconochie. If you told 'em as 'ow the war was goin' to end to-morrow they'd either call you a bloomin' liar, or grouse like 'ell becos they 'adn't 'ad the time to win the V.C.

"There was young Alf Cobb. 'E wasn't arf a grouser, an' 'e 'ad good luck all the bloomin' time. When 'e came to the front they put 'im along o' the transport becos 'e'd been a jockey before the war, an' 'e groused all the time that 'e didn't 'ave none of the fun of the fightin'. Fun of the fightin', indeed, when 'e'd got that little gal what we used to call Gertie less than ten minutes from the stables! She was a nice little bit of stuff, was Gertie, an', if only she'd spoke English instead of this bloomin' lingo what sounds like swearin' ..."

and here "Pongo" wandered off into a series of reminiscences of Gertie that have little to do with war and nothing to do with grumbling.

"'Owever, as I was sayin'," he continued at last, "that there Alf Cobb used to fair aggryvate me with 'is grousin'. When 'e got sent up for a spell in the trenches, and 'ad all 'the fun of the fightin',' 'e groused because 'e couldn't go off to some ole estaminet an' order 'is glass o' bitters like a dook. 'E groused becos 'e 'adn't got a feather bed, 'e groused becos 'e 'ad to cook 'is own food, an' 'e groused becos 'e didn't like the 'Uns. An' then when a whizz-bang landed on the parapet an' gave 'im a nice Blighty one in the arm, 'e groused becos 'e was afraid the sea'd be rough when 'e crossed over, an' 'e groused becos 'e couldn't light 'is own pipe. 'E's the sort of bloke what I don't like.

"What I like is a bloke like ole Lewis, who was always chirpy. 'E 'ad the rheumatics something fearful, but 'e never grumbled. Then 'e'd jest gone an' got spliced afore the war, an' 'is missis got 'im into debt an' then ran off with a fellow what works in the munitions. 'No good grousin',' says ole Joe Lewis, an' 'e still stayed cheerful, an' the night 'e 'eard as 'ow 'is young woman 'ad gone off 'e played away on 'is ole mouth-organ as 'appily as a fellow what's on 'is way to the Green Dragon with five bob in 'is pocket. The other blokes what knew about it thought as 'ow Joe didn't care at all, but I was 'is mate an' I knew as 'ow it 'urt a lot. When 'e got knocked over in that attack down Lee Bassey way, I jest stopped by 'im for a minute. 'Don't you worry about me, Pongo,' says 'e, 'I couldn't stand 'ome without 'er'—meanin' 'is missis, you see—'an' I'd rather 'op it like this. If I 'ad me ole mouth-organ 'ere, I'd give you chaps a tune to 'elp you on like.' That's the sort of bloke 'e was, chirpy up to the end. I 'ad to go on to the 'Un trenches, an' I never saw 'im again, for a big shell came along an' buried 'im.

"After all," continued "Pongo" after a pause, "it's a life what 'as its advantages. I ain't got to put on a 'ard collar o' Sundays out 'ere like me ole woman makes me do at 'ome. Then, I might 'ave stuck in that shell 'ole and 'ave been drowned; I might not 'ave 'ad a clean shirt to dry meself with; I might 'ave been 'it by a 'crump' yesterday. Yes, it might be worse, an' I ain't never a one to grouse."

Then someone who knew "Pongo" well made an apparently irrelevant remark. "There's plum and apple jam for rations again," he said.

"Pongo" rose to the fly at once. "Gawd!" he said, "if that ain't the bloomin' limit. I'd like to get me 'and round the neck of the bloke what gets all the raspberry an' apricot an' marmalade. 'Ere 'ave I been two years in the trenches, an' what 'ave I seen but plum an' apple? If it ain't plum an' apple, it's damson an' apple, which is jest the same only there's more stones in it. It do make me fair wild...."

"Pongo," insinuated someone at this moment, "I thought as 'ow you never grumbled."

"Pongo's" voice sank to its ordinary level. "That ain't grumblin'," he said. "I ain't a one to grumble."

But for the better part of an hour I heard him growling away to himself, and "plum and apple" was the burden of his growl. For even "Pongo" Simpson cannot always practise what he preaches.

XIII

THE CONVERT

John North, of the Non-Combatant Corps, leaned over the counter and smiled lovingly up into the shop girl's face. By an apparent accident, his hand slid across between the apple basket and the tins of biscuits, and came into gentle contact with hers. Knowing no French, his conversation was strictly limited, and he had to make amends for this by talking with his hand—by gently stroking her palm with his earth-stained thumb.

Mademoiselle Thérèse smiled shyly at him and her hand remained on the counter.

Private John North, thus encouraged, grew still bolder. He clasped her fingers in his fist, and was just wondering if he dared kiss them, when a gruff voice behind him caused him to stiffen, and to pretend he wanted nothing but a penny bar of chocolate.

"Now then, come orf it," said the newcomer, a private with the trench mud still caked on his clothes. "She's my young laidy, ain't yer, Thérèse?"

Thérèse smiled rather vaguely, for she knew no more Cockney than John North knew French.

"You clear out of 'ere," continued the linesman. "I don't want none o' you objector blokes 'anging around this shop, and if you come 'ere again I won't arf biff you one."

Unfortunately, it is the nature of woman to enjoy the sight of two men quarrelling for her favours, and Thérèse, guessing what was happening, was so unwise as to smile sweet encouragement at John North.

Even a Conscientious Objector loses his conscience when there is a woman in the case. John North turned up his sleeves as though he had been a boxer all his life, and proceeded to trounce his opponent with such vigour that the biscuit tins were hurled to the ground and the contents of a box of chocolates were scattered all over the floor.

As far as we are concerned, Mademoiselle Thérèse passes out of existence from this moment, but the little incident in her shop was not without consequences. In the first place, the Military Police cast the two miscreants into the same guard room, where, from bitter rivals, they became the best of friends. In the second place, John North, having once drawn blood, was no longer content with his former life, and wanted to draw more.

In the end he joined the Westfords, and fired his first shot over the parapet under direct tuition from his new friend. It matters little that his first shot flew several yards above the German parapet; the intention was good, and it is always possible that the bullet may have stung into activity some corpulent Hun whose duty called on him to lead pack horses about behind the firing line.

For weeks Holy John, as his company called him, passed out of my life. There were many other things to think of—bombs and grenades, attacks and counter-attacks, "barrages" and trench mortars, and all the other things about which we love to discourse learnedly when we come home on leave. John North was, for the time, completely forgotten.

But one day when the Great Push was in full swing, I met him again. From his former point of view he had sadly degenerated; from ours he had become a useful fellow with a useful conscience that told him England wanted him to "do in" as many Huns as he could.

I was supervising some work on a trench that had been German, but was now ours—the red stains on the white chalk told of the fight for it—when a voice I knew sounded from farther up the trench.

"If you don't bloomin' well march better, I won't arf biff you one, I won't," I heard, as the head of a strange little procession came round the traverse. At the rear of six burly but downcast Germans, came Private John North, late Conscientious Objector, driving his prisoners along with resounding oaths and the blood-chilling manœuvres of a bayonet that he brandished in his left hand.

"They'll all mine, sir, the beauties," he said as he passed me. "Got 'em all meself, and paid me little finger for 'em, too," and he held up a bandaged right arm for my inspection.

And, far down the trench, I heard him encouraging his prisoners with threats that would delight a pirate or a Chinaman.

How he, single-handed, captured six of the enemy I do not know, but he was the first man to reach the German wire, they tell me, and he brought in two wounded men from No Man's Land.

Personally, then, it hardly seems to me that six Germans are enough to pay for the little finger of Holy John, erstwhile Conscientious Objector.

XIV

DAVID AND JONATHAN

I

Strangely different though they were, they had been friends ever since they first met at school, eleven years before. Jonathan—for what other names are necessary than the obvious David and Jonathan?—was then a fat, sandy-haired boy, with a deep love of the country, and hands that, however often he washed them, always seemed to be stained with ink. He had a deep admiration, an adoration almost, for his dark-haired, dark-eyed David, wild and musical.

The love of the country it was that first made them friends, and David became, so to speak, Jonathan's means of expression, for David could put into words, and, later on, into music, what Jonathan could only feel dimly and vaguely. Jonathan was the typical British public-schoolboy with a twist of artistic sense hidden away in him, while David was possessed of a soul, and knew it. A soul is an awkward thing to possess at school in England, for it brings much "ragging" and no little contempt on its owner, and Jonathan fought many battles in defence of his less-understood friend.

Eleven years had wrought but little material change in them. Jonathan, after a few minor rebellions, had settled down in his father's office and was learning to forget the call of the open road and the half-formed dreams of his youth. David, on the other hand, was wandering over the Continent nominally studying languages for the Consular Service, really picking up a smattering of poetry, a number of friends, and a deep knowledge of music. From Jonathan, he had learned to hide his sentiments in the presence of those who would not understand, and to make his reason conquer the wilder of the whims that ran through his brain. Jonathan, in turn, had gained a power, which he scarcely realised, of appreciating music and scenery, and which no amount of office life would ever diminish.

Then the war broke out, and brought them together again.

At the beginning of it, David, who had been amusing himself in Madrid by teaching the elements of grammar and a large vocabulary of English slang to any Spaniard who would pay for it, came home and enlisted with Jonathan in a line regiment. For two months they drilled and exercised themselves in the so-called "arts of war." Then, chiefly on account of a soulless section commander, they applied for, and obtained, commissions in the same regiment.

In the same billet, they re-lived their schooldays, and over the fire in the evenings would call up old memories, or David would tell of his adventures abroad, until late in the night.

When the time came for them to go to the front, the Fates still favoured them; they went out together to the same regiment in France, and were drafted to the same company. Together they went up to the trenches for the first time, together they worked, together they crouched under the parapet when the German shells came unpleasantly close, and, all the time, Jonathan, calm and stolid, unconsciously helped the other, who, being cursed with a vivid imagination, secretly envied his friend's calm.

Now, nothing has more power to cement or break friendships than war. The enforced company, the sharing of danger, the common bearing of all imaginable discomforts combine to make comrades or enemies. There are so many things to tax one's patience, that a real friend in whom one may confide becomes doubly dear, while you end by hating a man who has the misfortune to irritate you day after day. War made David and Jonathan realise how much their friendship meant, and how necessary each was to the other, the one because of his continued calm, the other because of the relief his love of music and of Nature brought with it.

II

Near the end of April 1915 they came back to billets near Ypres. To the north a terrific battle was in progress, the last inhabitants were fleeing from the town, and huge shells screamed on their way, and burst with appalling clouds of smoke among the already shattered houses. Occasionally a motor cyclist would come racing down the road, and, once or twice, an ambulance came by with its load of gassed and wounded from the fighting to the north.

One morning, when the Germans seemed fairly quiet, David and Jonathan set out arm in arm towards Ypres, to explore. An occasional shell—a hum, increasing until it became a roar, followed, a moment after, by a fearful explosion—warned them not to proceed beyond the outskirts of the town, and here it was that they came upon a large villa, with lilac budding in the garden. By mutual consent, they turned in at the tall iron gate, and entered the half-ruined house.

The part of the house giving on the road had been destroyed by a large shell. Over a gaping hole in the ceiling was a bed, its iron legs weirdly twisted, which threatened to overbalance at any minute and to come hurtling down into the hall beneath. Shattered picture frames still hung on the walls, and on the floor near at hand lay a rosary, the Crucifix crushed by some heedless boot. The furniture lay in heaps, and the front door was lying grotesquely across a broken mirror. Everywhere was wreckage.

The other half of the house was still almost intact. In what had once been the salon they found comfortable chairs and an excellent Pleyel piano, while a copy of the *Daily Mirror* gave the clue that the room had until recently been occupied by British troops.

David seated himself at the piano and began to play, and Jonathan threw himself in an arm-chair near the window to listen, and to watch the alternate cloud and sunshine outside. It was one of those perfect mornings of April, bright-coloured and windy, and the breeze in the lilacs combined with the notes of the piano until they could hardly be told apart. The rare whirr and explosion of a shell only had the effect of accentuating the intervening peace. Jonathan had never felt so at one with Nature and with his friend, and more than once, stolid and calm though he generally was, he felt a tear in his eye at an extra beautiful little bit of music or the glory of the world outside.

III

"Coming up to the villa this morning?" asked David of his friend a day or two later.

"I've got a confounded rifle inspection at half-past ten. You go on and I'll get up there as soon as I can," answered Jonathan, and he went off to talk to his platoon sergeant while his friend strolled off to the villa.

When he was going up the road to Ypres an hour later, he met an orderly on horseback. "Excuse me, sir, I don't think the road's extry nice now," he said. "They're dropping some heavy stuff into Yips again."

Jonathan smiled. "Oh, that's all right," he said. "Thanks, all the same, for warning me. I'll take care." And he hurried on up the road.

It was not until he was inside the villa that he noticed anything out of the ordinary. Suddenly, however, he stopped aghast. The door by which they entered the salon was gone, and in its place was a huge gap in the wall. The furniture was buried under a mass of debris, and instead of the gilded ceiling above him was only the blue sky. The piano was still untouched, but on the keys, and on the wall behind, were splashes of blood. Lying on the ground near it, half covered in plaster, was David. He forced himself to approach, and looked again. His friend's head was completely smashed, and one arm was missing.

For some minutes he stood still, staring. Then, with a sudden quiver, he turned and ran. In the garden he tripped over something, and fell, but he felt no hurt, for mad terror was upon him, and all sense had gone. He must get away from the dreadful thing in there; he must put miles between himself and the vision; he must run ... run ... run....

IV

Two privates found him, wild-eyed and trembling, and brought him to a medical officer. "Nerves, poor devil, and badly too!" was the diagnosis; and before Jonathan really knew what had happened, he was in hospital in Rouen.

Everyone gets "nervy" after a certain amount of modern warfare; even the nerves of the least imaginative may snap before a sudden shock.

So with stolid Jonathan. After a year, he is still in England. "Why doesn't he go out again?" people ask. "He looks well enough. He must be slacking." But they realise nothing of the waiting at night for the dreaded, oft-repeated dreams; they cannot tell of the horrible visions that war can bring, they do not know what it means, that neurasthenia, that hell on earth.

It is difficult to forget what must be forgotten. If you have "nerves" you must do all you can to forget the things that caused them, but when everything you do or say, think or hear, reminds you in some remote way of all you must forget, then recovery is hard indeed.

That is why Jonathan is still in England. If he hears or reads of the war he thinks of his dead friend: if he hears music—even a street organ—the result is worse; if he tries to escape from it all, and hides himself away in the country, the birds and the lilac blossom take him back to that morning near Ypres, when he first realised how much his friendship meant to him. And whenever he thinks of his friend, that horrible corpse near the piano comes back before his tight-closed eyes, and his hands tremble again in fear.

XV

THE RUM JAR

AND OTHER SOLDIER SUPERSTITIONS

The most notable feature in the famous history of the "Angels of Mons" was the fact that hundreds of practical, unpoetical, and stolid English soldiers came forward and testified to having seen the vision. Whether the story were fact or fancy, it is an excellent example of a change in our national character.

Before the war, the unromantic Englishman who thought he saw a vision would have blamed in turn his eyesight, his digestion, his sobriety, and his sanity before he allowed that he had anything to do with the supernatural. He now tells, without the least semblance of a blush, that he puts his faith in superstitions, and charms, and mascots, and that his lucky sign has saved his life on half a dozen occasions.

Of all the many and weird superstitions that exist in the British Army of to-day, the most popular has to do with the jar that contains the ration of rum. Rumour has it that once, long ago, a party that was bringing up rations for a company in the trenches was tempted by the thought of a good drink, and fell. When all the rum had been consumed the question arose as to how to explain matters, and the genius of the party suggested breaking the jar and pretending that it had been hit by a bullet. When the party filed into the trench, the waiting company was shown the handle of the jar, and had to listen to a vivid tale of how a German bullet that had just missed Private Hawkes had wasted all the company's rum. Rumour also has it that the unsteady gait of one member of the party gave the lie to the story—but this is beside the point.

From this little incident there has sprung up a far-reaching superstition—German bullets, the men have it, swerve instinctively towards the nearest rum jar. A few stray shots have helped to strengthen the belief, and the conviction holds firm down nearly the whole length of the British line that the man who carries the rum jar runs a double risk of being hit.

Mascots and talismans hold an important place in the soldier's life. I know of one man who used to carry in his pack a rosary that he had picked up in one of the streets of Ypres. One day his leg was fractured in two places by a large piece of a trench-mortar bomb, but, in spite of his pain, he refused to be taken down to the dressing station until we had hunted through his pack and found him his rosary. "If I don't take it with me," he said, "I'll get 'it again on the way down."

And this is by no means an isolated example. Nearly every man at the front has a mascot of some sort—a rosary, a black cat, a German button, or a weird sign—which is supposed to keep him safe.

Their superstitions, too, are many in number. One man is convinced that he will be killed on a Friday; another man would rather waste a dry—and therefore valuable—match than light three cigarettes with it; another will think himself lucky if he can see a cow on his way up to the trenches; a fourth will face any danger, volunteer for any patrol, go through the worst attack without a qualm, simply because he "has got a feeling he will come through unhurt." And he generally does, too.

I once had a servant who used to wear a shoe button on a piece of string round his neck. At some village billet in France a tiny girl had given it him as a present, and he treasured it as carefully as a diamond merchant would treasure the great Koh-i-noor stone—in fact, I am convinced that he often went without washing just to avoid the risk of loss in taking it off and putting it on again. To you in England it seems ridiculous that a man should hope to preserve his life by wearing a shoe button on a piece of string. But then, you have not seen the strange tricks that Fate will play with lives. You have not watched how often a shell will burst in a group of men, kill one outright, and leave the others untouched; you have not joked with a friend one moment and knelt by him to catch his dying words the next; you have not stood at night by a hastily dug grave and wondered, as you mumbled a few half-remembered prayers, why the comrade who is lying there on a waterproof sheet should have been killed while you are left unhurt.

Besides, there are so many things which tend to make a man superstitious and to confirm him in his trust in mascots and charms. Many a man has had a premonition of his death, many a man has come through long months of war, and then has been killed on the day on which he lost his mascot.

The thought of superstition recalls to me Joe Williams, the ex-policeman. Joe Williams was a fatalist, and believed every word he read in his little book of prophecies, so that the dawn of September 4th found him glum and depressed.

"It ain't no bloomin' good," he grumbled. "It says in my book as 'ow September 4th is a disastrous day for England, so it will be. There ain't no way of stopping Fate." And when his section laughed at him for his fears he merely shrugged his shoulders, and sat gazing into the brazier's glow.

The day wore quietly on, and I had forgotten all about Williams and his gloomy prophecies when a corporal came along to my dug-out. "Williams has been hit by a bomb, sir," he said, "and is nearly done for."

At the other end of the trench lay Joe Williams, near to death, while his comrades tied up his wounds. The glumness had gone from his face, and when he saw me he signed for me to stoop down. "What did I tell you, sir, about the disaster for England?" he whispered. "Ain't this a bloomin' disaster?" and he tried to laugh at his little joke, but the flow of blood choked him, and he died.

Perhaps, though, he was nearer the mark than he imagined, for it is a rash thing to say that the death of a man who can joke with his dying breath is not a disaster to England.

It may all seem intensely foolish to you, and childish; it may strike you that our men at the front are attempting to bribe Fate, or that we are returning to the days of witches and sorcerers. But it is not without its good points, this growth of superstition. Man is such a little, helpless pawn in the ruthless game of war, and death is so sudden and so strange, that the soul gropes instinctively in search of some sign of a shielding arm and a watchful power. The Bible, the Crucifix, a cheap little charm—any of these may bring comfort to the man in the trench, and give him the illusion that he is not one of those marked for the sickle of Death.

A man who is confident that he will come through a battle unhurt generally does so, or, if Death comes, he meets it with a smile on his lips. The man who expects to be killed, who has no belief in some shielding power—though it be but symbolised by a common shoe button—is taken by Death very soon, but, even then, not before he has gone through those long, morbid hours of waiting that breed the germs of fear.

The penny lucky charm that can bring comfort to a man in danger is not a thing to be ridiculed. It may be a proof of ignorance, but to the man it is symbolical of his God, and is therefore worthy of all respect and reverence from others.

XVI

THE TEA SHOP

Baker came to me directly after lunch. "Look here," he said, "I'm not satisfied."

"What's the matter now?"

"I want something respectable to eat. Let's go into Poperinghe and get a properly cooked tea."

"It's six miles," I objected, "and a confoundedly hot day."

"All the better for an omelette appetite."

I thought of the omelettes in the tea shop of Poperinghe, and I knew that I was lost. "Can't you get horses?" I asked.

"No luck. The transport has to shift to-day and there's nothing doing in that line. I asked just before lunch."

The omelettes danced up and down before my eyes until the intervening miles over hard cobble stones dwindled to nothing. "All right," I said. "Will you go and get leave for us? I'll be ready in a minute." And I went off to borrow some money from Jackson with which to pay for my omelettes.

The church tower of Poperinghe shimmered in the heat and seemed to beckon us on along the straight road that led through the miles of flat country, relieved here and there by stretches of great hop poles or by little red-roofed farms where lounged figures in khaki.

In every field grazed dozens of horses and in every lane were interminable lines of motor lorries, with greasy-uniformed men crawling about underneath them or sleeping on the seats. In one place, a perspiring "Tommy" hurried round a farmyard on his hands and knees, and barked viciously for the benefit of a tiny fair-haired girl and a filthy fox-terrier puppy; and right above him swung a "sausage" gleaming in the sunlight. Just outside Poperinghe we met company after company of men, armed with towels, waiting by the roadside for baths in the brewery, and, as we passed, one old fellow, who declared that his "rheumatics was that bad he couldn't wash," was trying to sell a brand-new cake of soap for the promise of a drink.

The sun was hot in the sky, and the paving, than which nothing on earth is more tiring, seemed rougher and harder than usual; motor lorries, or cars containing generals, seemed, at every moment, to compel us to take to the ditch, and we were hot and footsore when we tramped through the Grande Place to the tea shop.

But here we were doomed to disappointment, for not a chair was vacant—"Not room for a flea," as Madame explained to us, and we had to curb our appetites as best we could.

The tea shop at Poperinghe! Where could you hope to find a more popular spot than was the tea shop in the early part of 1915? Where could you get better omelettes served by a more charming little waitress?—was she really charming, I wonder, or did she merely seem so *faute de mieux*? Where could you find a nicer place to meet your friends from other regiments, to drink coffee, to eat quantities of dainty French cakes? It is not surprising that the shop at Poperinghe was always crowded by four in the afternoon in those old days before the second battle of Ypres.

As patiently as might be, Baker and I waited, lynx-eyed, until two chairs were vacated.

"Mademoiselle," we called, "deux omelettes, s'il vous plait."

"Bien, messieurs, tout de suite."

But we were far too hungry to wait, and before the omelettes arrived we had cleared a great plate of cakes. After weeks of indifferent trench cooking the first well-done omelette is a great joy, and, as I put down my fork, I glanced inquiry at Baker.

"Rather," he answered to my unspoken question.

"Mademoiselle, encore deux omelettes, s'il vous plait," I ordered. "Nous avons une faim de loup."

"Je m'en aperçois, messieurs les officiers," answered our fair enchantress, as she hurried off to repeat our order in the kitchen, while a crowd of predatory officers glared murder at us when they found we did not intend to leave our places so soon. "Some fellows are pigs," murmured one.

"That was splendid," said Baker when we started off on our homeward walk. "But six miles is a hell of a long way."

Personally, though, I enjoyed those six miles through the dusk, for we seemed to hear the hum of the traffic and the shouts of newsboys. Our tea brought back souvenirs of England, and we talked of London and of home, of theatres, and of coast patrol on the southern cliffs, until the little low huts of our camp showed up ahead.

It is nearly two years now since Baker was killed. He was found gassed in a dug-out on Hill 60, and by his side lay his servant, who had died in the attempt to drag him out to the comparative safety of the open trench. Nearly two years since another friend gave up his life for his country; nearly two years since another mother in England learned that her son had been killed in a "slight diversion on the Ypres salient"!

But it was thus that he would have wished to die.

XVII

"HERE COMES THE GENERAL"

A servant brought me a note to my dug-out:

"Come down and have some lunch in trench 35D," it ran, "in C Company officers' dug-out. Guests are requested to bring their own plates and cutlery; and, if it is decent, their own food. Menu attached. R.S.V.P."

The menu was as follows:

MENU OF LUNCHEON GIVEN BY C COMPANY AT THEIR COUNTRY RESIDENCE, "THE RETREAT," 15/5/15.

SOUPS

Soup à la Bully Beef.   Soup à l'Oxo.

FISH

Salmon (and Shrimp Paste) without Mayonnaise Sauce.
Sardines à l'Huile (if anyone provides them).

ENTREES

Maconochie, very old.
Bully beef and boiled potatoes.

SWEETS

Pineapple Chunks, fresh from the tin.
English Currant Cake.

SAVOURY

Welsh Rarebit.

I read through the menu, and decided to risk it, and, procuring the necessary crockery, I clanked through fully half a mile of trenches to C Company. The officers' dug-out was in the cellar of an old cottage which just came in our line of trenches. The only access to it was by means of a very narrow stairway which led down from the trench. The interior, when I arrived, was lit by three candles stuck in bottles, which showed officers in almost every vacant spot, with the exception of one corner, where a telephone orderly was situated with his apparatus. I occupied the only untenanted piece of ground I could find, and awaited events.

The soup was upset, as the moment when the servant was about to bring it down from the outer air was the moment chosen for a rehearsal of that famous game, "Here comes the General." The rules of this game are simple. The moment anyone utters the magic phrase there is an immediate rush for the steps, the winner of the game being he who manages to arrive at the top first and thus impress the imaginary general with his smartness.

The soup stood but a poor chance in a stampede of eleven officers, the candles were kicked out, and a long argument ensued as to whose plate was which, and why Martin's spoon should have gone down Fenton's neck, and if the latter should be made to forfeit his own spoon to make up for his unintentional theft.

Order was at length restored, and the meal was proceeding in comparative peace, when, suddenly, Jones, who had not been invited to the luncheon, appeared at the top of the steps.

"I say, you fellows," he cried excitedly. "Here comes the General."

"Liar!" shouted someone. But the magic words could not be allowed to pass unnoticed, even though we were eating pineapple chunks at the time, and they are very sticky if you upset them over your clothes.

A fearful scramble took place, in which everyone—with the exception of Walters, who placed himself in the further corner with the tin of pineapple— tried to go together up steps which were just broad enough to allow the passage of one man at a time.

A conglomerate mass of officers, all clinging convulsively to each other, suddenly burst into the open trench—almost at the feet of the General, who came round the traverse into view of them at that moment.

When I returned to C Company's dug-out, an hour or so later, to try to recover my plate and anything else that had not been smashed, I found three officers reading a message that had just come by telephone from Battalion Headquarters. It was prefixed by the usual number of mysterious letters and figures and ran:

"The Brigadier has noticed with regret the tendency of several officers to crowd into one dug-out. This practice must cease. An officer should have his dug-out as near those of his own men as possible, and should not pass his time in the dug-outs belonging to officers of other companies."

"Here comes the General!" whispered somebody.

I got first up the steps and hurried, a battered plate in my hand, along the trenches to my dug-out.

XVIII

THE RASCAL IN WAR

Even the most apathetic of us has been changed by war—he who in times of peace was content with his ledgers and daily office round is now in the ranks of men who clamber over the parapet and rush, cheering, to the German lines; she who lived for golf, dances, and theatres is now caring for the wounded through the long nights in hospital. Everyone in every class of life has altered—the "slacker" has turned soldier, and the burglar has become a sound, honest man.

Strange it is that war, which might be expected to arouse all the animal passions in us, has done us so much good! There are among the men in the trenches many hundreds who were, before the war, vastly more at home in the police courts and prisons than is the average Londoner at a public dinner. That they should be brave is not astonishing, for adventure is in their bones, but they are also as faithful, as trustworthy, as amenable to discipline as any soldiers we possess.

There was "Nobby" Clarke, for instance. "Nobby" was a weedy little Cockney who became my "batman," or servant. He had complete control of my privy purse, did all my shopping, and haggled over my every halfpenny as carefully as though it were his own. Then, when he had served me for over six months, I overheard him one day recounting his prison experiences, and I discovered that he had been a pilferer and pickpocket well known in all the London police courts. In his odd moments out of jail, he would hover outside the larger stations, touch a bedraggled cap with a filthy finger, and say, "Kerry yer beg, sir?" in a threatening tone to all passers-by; his main income, however, appeared to come from far less respectable sources.

And yet he served me more faithfully than I have ever been served before or since, and I have seldom been more sorry than I was when "Nobby" Clarke was hit. As we were tying him up—he had been wounded in eight places by a rifle grenade—he signed to me and I stooped over him.

"I ain't got no one at 'ome as cares fer me," he said, "so yer might 'and me things round to the blokes 'ere. I've got a photograph of me ole woman wot died five years ago. It's in me pay book, sir, an' I'd like yer to keep it jest to remind yer of me." Then, his voice getting weaker every moment, "I ain't been such a bad servant to yer, 'as I, sir?" he whispered, his eyes looking appealingly into mine. And when "Nobby" Clarke, onetime loafer and pickpocket, passed away, I am not ashamed to own that there was a queer sort of lump in my throat.

And he was only one of many, was "Nobby" Clarke. There was Bennett, the tramp, who was always ready with a song to cheer up the weary on the march; there was a Jewish money-lender who was killed while trying to save a man who was lying wounded in No Man's Land; there was Phillips, who had been convicted of manslaughter—he became a stretcher-bearer, and was known all over the battalion for his care of the wounded.

In every regiment in every army you will find a little group of men who were tramps and beggars and thieves, and, almost without exception, they have "made good." For the first time in their lives they have been accepted as members of great society, and not driven away as outcasts. The Army has welcomed them, disciplined them, and taught them the elements of self-respect—a quality whose very existence they ignored before the war.

There is an Italian proverb—"Tutto il mondo è paese"—which means, in its broadest sense, "All the world is ruled by the same passion and qualities." In the old days it needed a Dickens, and, later, a Neil Lyons to discover the qualities of the criminal classes; now war has brought us all together—the erstwhile city merchant warms himself before the same brazier as the man who would have picked his pocket three years before—and we suddenly find that we are no better than the beggar, and that a man who stole apples from a stall is no worse at heart than the inhabitant of Mayfair.

It is not that our ideas of greatness have degenerated when we call these men heroes; it is not that war is entirely a thing of evil, so that the criminal shines as a warrior—it is that these "outcasts" have changed. Statistics prove that crime has decreased since the war began, and crime will continue to decrease, for that indefinable instinct we call patriotism has seized on all classes alike, so that the criminal can make the supreme sacrifice just as magnificently as the man who has "kept straight" all his life.

And the best of it is that this reform among burglars and beggars is not for the "duration of the war only." War has lost us our sons and our fathers, it has brought appalling sorrow and suffering into the world, but it has given the very poor a chance they have never had before. No more are they outcasts; they are members of society, and such they will remain. If this were all the good that war could do, it would still be our ultimate gain that the great scourge is passing over the world.

XIX

"PONGO" SIMPSON ON OFFICERS

"Orficers," said "Pongo" Simpson, "is rum blokes. I've got a fam'ly of six kids back at 'ome, not counting Emma what's in service, an' I reckon my orficer's more trouble to look after nor all the lot of 'em put together. It's always: 'Simpson, where the dooce is my puttees?' or 'Simpson, you've sewed this 'ere button on in the wrong place,' or 'Simpson, the soup tastes like cocoa and the cocoa tastes like soup'—does 'e expect me to kerry a bloomin' collection of canteens? Don't 'e think it better to 'ave cocoa what's got a bit o' soup in it than to 'ave a canteen what's been washed in a shell 'ole along of a dead 'Un? Why, if we was goin' to charge to Berlin to-morrer I'd 'ave to spend 'arf the night cleanin' 'is boots and buttons.

"Yes, 'e's a funny sort o' bloke, my orficer, but, my Gawd!"—and here Simpson expectorated to give emphasis to his statement—"I'd foller 'im against a crowd of 'Uns, or a lot of wimmen what's waiting for their 'usbands what ain't come 'ome at three in the morning, or anythink else you like. 'E's an 'elpless sort of chap, an' 'e's got funny ideas about shavin' and washin'—sort of disease, you know—but 'e's a good sort when you knows 'is little ways.

"Do you remember that young Mr. Wilkinson?" asked "Pongo," and a few of the "old hands" in the dug-out nodded affirmatively. "'E was a one, 'e was," resumed "Pongo." "Do you remember the day we was gassed on 'Ill 60? 'E used to be my bloke then, and I was with 'im all the time. 'E was a proper lad! When the gas 'ad gone over there was only five of A Company left, with 'im in charge, and we knew as 'ow the 'Uns would attack as soon as they thought we was properly wiped out. And Mr. Wilkinson was fine. All down the trench 'e put blokes' rifles on the parapet, and the 'ole bloomin' six of us ran up an' down the trench like a lot of rabbits, firin' off rifle after rifle till the Alleymans must 'ave thought we was an 'ole battalion. The only times when Mr. Wilkinson wasn't firin' rifles, 'e was fusin' bombs, jest as busy as that little girl be'ind the counter of the Nag's 'Ead of a Saturday night. 'E must 'ave sent a good number of 'Uns 'ome that day with bits of bombs inside of them.

"And you should 'a' seen Mr. Wilkinson when the Sergeant wos for givin' in and goin' back to the second line! We'd all the gas in us more or less, and 'e could 'ardly talk, 'e was that bad, but when 'e 'eard the Sergeant say as 'ow 'e was goin' back, 'e shouted like the Colonel on a battalion parade. 'Curse you, Sergeant!' 'e yelled, 'what's the good of goin' back? We've got to 'old this trench or 'op it. If you don't like the air down there, come up on the parapet with me.' And up 'e jumps on to the parapet with the gas clearin' away, and the Fritzes only 30 or 40 yards off.

"'It? Why, of course 'e was 'it. 'E was laughin' like a kid what's stealin' apples—all excited like—when they got 'im right through the 'ead, and 'e fell down on the other side of the parapet. But 'e'd done what 'e wanted to, for the Sergeant wasn't talkin' any more about goin' back. 'E crawled out over the parapet and brought poor Mr. Wilkinson back, and got 'it in the leg while 'e was doin' it, too. But that didn't matter to 'im, for 'e was out to 'ave 'is own back, was the Sergeant, and we 'eld that bloomin' trench for another hour until the blokes got up the communication trench to 'elp us. There's a lot of medals what ought to go to blokes as don't get them, and it might 'ave 'elped Mr. Wilkinson's mother if they'd given 'im the V.C., but there weren't no other orficers about, and they didn't take any notice of us chaps."

"Talkin' of 'Ill 60," said Bert Potter, "there was that Captain—I misremember 'is name—you know, that bloke what got into trouble at the ole farm for giving a cow a tin o' bully beef, and the cow died next day. I was in 'is trench with a machine gun when 'e got 'is little bit. A chunk out of an 'and grenade 'it 'im in the thigh, and 'e laughed like 'ell becos 'e'd got a 'cushy' wound. Why, 'e even said as 'ow 'e could walk down to the dressing station, and we envied 'im like 'ell and thought it was only a flesh wound. I got 'it the next day and went to the same 'orspital where 'e was. 'E'd 'ad 'is thigh bone smashed all to bits, and they'd jest taken 'is leg off when I saw 'im. 'E was weak as a kid and chirpy as a sparrer, and only cursin' becos 'e was out of things for the rest of the war. I never 'eard what 'appened to 'im, but the nurse told me as 'ow they was afraid 'e wouldn't recover becos of emmyridge, or something with a name like that. And 'e wasn't more nor twenty-one years old neither, pore bloke."

"But you won't beat the Medical Orficer anywhere," said Jones, one of the stretcher-bearers who was on duty in the trenches. "'E don't 'ave to fight, but you should see 'im when things is busy up 'ere. Coat off an' sleeves up, workin' for 'ours on end till any man what wasn't an 'orse would drop dead. 'E's 'ard on the shirkers and scrimshankers—e's the sort of bloke what would give you a dose o' castor oil for earache or frost-bitten feet, but 'e's like a mother with the wounded. I've seen 'im, too, goin' along the cutting when the whizz-bangs was burstin' all the way down it, carryin' some wounded fellow in 'is arms as calmly as if 'e were an ole girl carryin' a parcel along Regent Street. And then," said Jones, as he named the greatest point in the M.O.'s favour, "'e's the best forward on a wet day as ever I seed."

Just at that moment a voice sounded from farther up the trench. "Simpson," it said, "where the deuce is my toothbrush?"

"Jest comin', sir. I've got 'un," answered "Pongo" Simpson as he produced a greasy-looking toothbrush from his pocket. "'Ere, give us that canteen of 'ot water," he said quietly, "I used 'is toothbrush to grease 'is boots with yesterday—didn't think 'e'd miss it, for you don't come out 'ere to wash your teeth. They 'ave got funny ways, these 'ere orficers. 'Owever," he continued as he wiped the brush dry on the sleeve of his tunic, "what the eye don't see, the 'eart don't grieve over. 'E'll only think as 'ow it's the water what's greasy."

"Simpson," came the voice from farther along the trench, a moment or so later, "this is the greasiest water I've ever tasted. What the deuce you've done to it I don't know."

XX

THE HAND OF SHADOW

"Come in," said Margery Debenham, as she opened her eyes lazily to the sunlight. "Put my tea on the table, please, Mary. I'm too sleepy to drink it yet.

"There's a letter from the front, miss," said Mary with emphasis, as she went out of the room.

Margery was awake in a second. She jumped out of bed, slipped on a dressing-gown, and, letter in hand, ran over to the window to read it in the morning sunshine. As she tore open the envelope and found only a small sheet of paper inside, she made a little *moue* of disappointment, but the first words of the letter changed it into a sigh of joy. It was dated September 13th and ran:

"MY DARLING,

"At last I have got my leave, and am coming home to be married. Our months of waiting are over. I leave here to-morrow afternoon, shall spend the night on the way somewhere, and shall arrive in London late on the 15th, or during the morning of the 16th. I must spend the day in town to do a little shopping (I couldn't be seen at my own wedding very well in the clothes I have on now) and expect to get down to Silton at 3.20 on the 17th. I have to be back in this hole on the 24th, so that if we get married on Saturday we shall have quite a nice little honeymoon. Darling little one! Isn't it too good to be true? I can hardly realise that within a week I shall be

"Your devoted and hen-pecked husband

RONALD."

"P.S.—I have written to father, and he will make all arrangements for Saturday.

"P.P.S.—Shall I be allowed to smoke in the drawing-room?"

Margery Debenham leant out of the window and gazed at the garden and the orchard beyond. The light flickered through the trees of the old flagged path along which she and Ronald had so often wandered, and she could just see the tall grass waving down at the bottom of the orchard, where they used to sit and discuss the future. Everything reminded her of her lover who was coming back to her, who would be with her again to-morrow afternoon. At the thought of the five long, weary months of waiting that were passed, and of the eight days of happiness that were coming, two little tears crept out of her eyes and down her cheeks. She brushed them impatiently away, for she was too busy to cry. She must run and tell her parents; she must hurry over to talk to Ronald's father; she must write to her friends; she must run down to the bottom of the orchard and watch for a while the trout that lay in the little stream; she must laugh and sing until the whole village of Silton knew that her waiting was over, and that Ronald was in England again.

Captain Ronald Carr hoisted his pack on his shoulder, and turned to three officers who were looking at him enviously. "Cheer oh, you fellows," he said, "think of me in two days' time, while you are being 'strafed' by the Hun, rushing about town in a taxi," and, with a wave of his hand, he marched off to battalion headquarters, followed by Butler, his servant. From battalion headquarters he had a distance of two miles to walk to the cross roads where he was to meet his groom with his horse, but the day was hot and progress was rather slow. His first quarter of a mile was along a narrow and winding communicating trench; after that the way was along a hidden road, but huge shell craters all along told that the German artillery had it well marked.

Away to the right a bombardment was in progress, and the dull thuds of the guns came sleepily through the September haze; above him, a skylark sang lustily; the long grass by the roadside smelt sweet and lush. As Ronald Carr strode down the road, he laughed to himself at the fairness of the world.

Of a sudden, a shell burst over some trees a few hundred yards away, and, as the white smoke rolled away, he felt aware of a change.

Supposing he were to get wounded on the way down! With the next warning whine of a coming shell he found himself ducking as never before, for Captain Carr was not a man who often crouched for nothing.

Another shell came, and another, and with each his feeling grew. Just so must a mouse feel, he thought, when a cat plays with it. He felt as though he were at the mercy of an enormous giant, and that, each time he thought to escape, the shadow of a huge hand fell on the ground around him, and he knew that the hand above was waiting to crush him. At the thought, the hair on his forehead grew damp; time after time he checked his mad impulse to quicken his pace, and caught himself glancing covertly at his servant to see if he noticed his captain's strange behaviour. Suppose the hand should crush him before he could get back to England, to his home, to his marriage!

Suddenly there were four short, loud hisses, and four shells burst along the road close in front of them.

"They're searching the road. Quick, into the ditch," shouted Carr to his servant, as he jumped into an old trench that ran along the roadside. Butler turned to do the same, slipped on the *pavé*, and fell heavily, his ankle badly sprained. Those hateful hisses would come again before the man could crawl into safety, and this time they would probably be nearer, and escape almost miraculous. Captain Carr leaped out of the trench again and helped his servant to his feet.

"Cling on to me, man!" and, a moment after, he shouted, "down, here they come again!" and they flung themselves on their faces scarce two feet from the ditch and probable safety.

When Butler raised his head again after the four explosions, Captain Ronald Carr lay at his side, dead. The hand had grasped its prey.

Margery Debenham was standing in front of her mirror, getting ready to go to meet Ronald by the 3.20 train, when Mr. Carr came to announce the receipt of the War Office telegram.

She could find no tears when she heard the news; she felt stunned, and vaguely bored by the platitudes of consolation people uttered. When she could escape, she went slowly down the flagged path, where they used to walk to the orchard, where the future had been planned by two people full of the happy confidence of the young. She flung herself down in the long grass by the stream, and buried her hot face in her hands.

"What does it all mean?" she said to herself. Then, a minute later, she thought of all the other women who had to bear the same pain, and all for no reason. "There is no God," she cried passionately. "No one can help me, for there is no God." Day after day, night after night of waiting, and all for nothing. All those hours of agony, when the papers talked of "diversions" on the British front, rewarded by the supreme agony, by the sudden loss of all hope. No more need to hunt for a loved but dreaded name through the casualty lists every morning; all that was finished now.

The splash of a jumping trout in the pool under the willow tree took her thoughts away from her pain for the fraction of a second—just sufficient time to allow the soothing tears to come.

"O God," she murmured, "help me to see why. Help me, God, help me!" and she burst into sobs, her face pressed down into the cool, long grass.

XXI

THE VETERAN

Old Jules Lemaire, ex-sergeant in the 3rd regiment of the line, raised his wine glass.

"Bonne chance," he said, "and may you fight the devils as we did in 1870 and 1871, and with more success too."

"Enough of you and your 1870," said someone roughly. "We go out to win where you lost; there will be no Woerth or Sedan in this war. We will drive the Prussians back to Berlin; you let them march to Paris. We are going to act, whereas you can only talk—you are much too old, you see, Père Lemaire."

The ex-sergeant put down his glass with a jerk as though he had been struck. He looked around on the company that filled the front room of the Faisan d'Or, and on the faces of the men who had looked up to him for years as the hero of 1870 he now saw only the keenness to fight. He was old, forgotten, and no longer respected, and the blow was a hard one to bear.

The cloud of war was drifting up from the east, and the French Army was mobilising for the Great War. The peasants of the village had just been called up, and within half an hour they would be on their way to the depots of their different regiments, while Jules Lemaire, sergeant of the line, would be left at home with the cripples and the women and the children.

"I will serve France as well as any of you," he said defiantly. "I will find a way." But his voice was unheeded in the general bustle and noise, and Madame Nolan, the only person who appeared to hear him, sniffed with contempt.

Men destined for different regiments were saying good-bye to each other; Georges Simon, the blacksmith, with his arm round his fiancée's waist, was joking with Madame Nolan, who hurried about behind her little zinc counter; the door slammed noisily at each departure—and Jules Lemaire sat unheeded in the corner by the old clock.

And presently, when the front room was quiet and Madame Nolan was using her dirty apron to wipe away her tears, the ex-sergeant crept out quietly into the street and hobbled along to his cottage. He reached up and took his old Chassepot rifle down from the wall where it had hung these many years, and, while the other inhabitants thronged the road, cheering, weeping, laughing, Jules Lemaire sat before his little wooden table, with his rifle in his hands and a pile of cartridges before him.

"There will be a way," he murmured. "I will help my country; there will be a way."

The grey invaders swept on through the village, and Jules Lemaire, from his hiding-place on the church tower, watched them come with tears of impotent rage on his cheeks. Battalion after battalion they passed by—big, confident Germans who jeered at the peasants, and who sang as they plodded over the *pavé*. Once, when a company was halted beneath him, while the officers went in to the Faisan d'Or across the road, to see what they could loot in the way of drinks, the ex-sergeant aimed carefully at the captain, but he put down his rifle without firing.

At last, late in the afternoon when the dusk was beginning to hide the southern hills, Jules Lemaire's waiting came to an end. A large motor car drew up outside the inn, and a general with three officers of his staff got out into the road. One of the officers spread a map on the old door bench—where Jules Lemaire had so often sat of an evening and told of his adventures in the war—and, while an orderly went to procure wine for them, the four Germans bent over the plan of the country they thought to conquer.

Suddenly a shot rang out from the church tower above them. The general fell forward on to the bench, while his blood and his wine mingled in a staining stream that ran across the map of invincible France, and dripped down on to the dust below.

They met Jules Lemaire coming down the spiral steps of the church tower, his rifle still in his hand. They hit him with their rifle butts, they tied him up with part of the bell rope, and propped him up against the church wall.

Just before they fired, Jules Lemaire caught sight of Madame Nolan, who stood, terrified and weeping, at the doorway of the inn.

"You see," he shouted to her, "I also, I have helped my country. I was not too old after all."

And he died with a smile on his face.

XXII

THE SING-SONG

As soon as the battalion marches back from the trenches to the village in the first light of the morning, everyone turns his mind to methods which will help the few days of rest to pass as pleasantly as war and the limited amusements afforded by two estaminets and a row of cottages will permit.

"Chacun son goût." As he tramps along the street, B Company Sergeant-Major challenges Corporal Rogers to a boxing match on the morrow; Second Lieutenant White, who is new to war, sits in his billet and, by the light of a candle stuck in a bottle, traces the distance to the nearest town on the off chance that he will get leave to visit it; the doctor demands of his new landlady, in the most execrable French, where he can find a field suitable for "le football"; and Private Wilson, as he "dosses down" on the floor, suggests sleepily to Private Jones that he will be thirsty in the afternoon and that Private Jones has been owing him a drink since that day in Ouderdom three weeks ago.

Besides such methods of passing the time, there are baths to be had in the great brewery vats of the village, there is an inter-company hockey tournament to be played with a Tickler's jam tin in lieu of a ball, and, best of all, there is the "sing-song."

Be it in a trench, or in a barn, or out in the open fields where the battalion lies bivouacked under rows of waterproof sheets strung up as inadequate tents, the sing-song is sure of success, and a man with a voice like a mowing machine will receive as good a reception as would Caruso or Melba at Covent Garden. There is a French Territorial regiment which has a notice up at the entrance of its "music hall"—"Entrée pour Messieurs les Poilus. Prix un sourire." Admission a smile! There is never a man turned away from its doors, for where is the "poilu" or where is the "Tommy" who is not always ready with a smile and a laugh and a song?

There are little incidents in life that engrave themselves deep in the memory. Of all the sing-songs I have attended, there is one that is still vivid—the brush of time has washed away the outlines and edges of the others.

We were billeted, I remember, in Eliza's farm—Eliza, for the benefit of those who do not know her, is fair, fat, fifty, and Flemish; a lady who shakes everyone in the farm into wakefulness at five o'clock each morning by the simple process of stepping out of bed—when the Captain decided that we wanted "taking out of ourselves." "We'll have a sing-song," he announced.

So the Company Sergeant-Major was called in to make arrangements, and at eight o'clock that evening we wandered into the Orchestra Stalls. The concert hall was a large barn with a double door in the middle which had been opened wide to allow the admittance of a cart, which was placed in the entrance to act as a stage. All around the high barn, and perched precariously on the beams, were the men, while we of the Orchestra Stalls were accommodated on chairs placed near the stage. Behind the cart was a background consisting of Eliza and her numerous gentlemen friends, her daughter, an old lady aged roughly a hundred, and a cow that had no right to be there at all, but had wandered in from the nearest field to see the show. An orchestral accompaniment was kept up, even during the saddest recitation, by dozens of little pigs that scrambled about in the farmyard and under the stage. And beyond the farm swayed the tall poplars that stood along the road which led straight away into the distance, whence came sudden flashes of light and the long, dull rumble of the guns.

Of the programme itself, I have but the vaguest recollection, for the programmes are the least interesting part of these performances. The first item, I remember, was a dreadful sentimental song by Private Higgs which accident converted from comparative failure into howling success. Just as he was rendering the most affecting passage, Private Higgs stepped back too far, the cart—of the two-wheeled variety—overbalanced, and the sad singer was dropped down amongst the little pigs below, to the great joy of the crowd.

Then came a Cockney humorist, who, in times of peace, was the owner of a fried fish and chip barrow in that home of low comedians—the East End. After him appeared Sergeant Andrews, disguised in one of Eliza's discarded skirts, with a wisp of straw on his head to represent a lady's hair. Some vulgar song he sang in a shrill, falsetto voice that caused great dismay among the pigs, as yet unused to the vagaries of the British soldier.

After the interval, during which the audience *en masse* made a pilgrimage to Eliza's back door to buy beer at a penny a glass, there came the usual mixture of the vulgar and the sentimental, for nothing on earth is more sentimental than a soldier. There was the inevitable "Beautiful Picture in a Beautiful Golden Frame," and a recitation in Yiddish which was well applauded simply because no man had any idea what it was about. The Sergeant-Major gave a very creditable rendering of "Loch Lomond" in a voice that would terrify a recruit, and we finished up the evening with a song requesting a certain naughty boy to hold out his hand, which was shouted by everyone with so much vigour that one wondered how it was the men could still sing "God save the King" when the time came.

And far into the night, when the farmyard lay still and ghostly, and the pigs had gone off to bed, we still sat and talked in the "Officers' Mess," and recalled jokes of George Robey and Harry Tate, or hummed over the tunes we had heard at the last Queen's Hall concert. As the Captain had said, we wanted "taking out of ourselves," and it had just needed an impromptu concert in an old Flemish barn to do it.

———————————————————————————————————————

XXIII

THE "STRAFE" THAT FAILED

There is a certain battery in France where the name of Archibald Smith brings a scowl to every brow and an oath to every lip. The Battery Major still crimsons with wrath at the thought of him, and the Observing Officer remembers bitterly the long, uncomfortable hours he spent, perched up in a tree a hundred yards or so from the German lines. And this is how Archibald Smith was the unwitting cause of so much anger to the battery, and the saver of many a German life.

One morning shortly before dawn the Commanding Officer of an infantry regiment was wading down a communicating trench, when he met an artillery officer, accompanied by three men with a big roll of telephone wire.

"Hullo, what are you doing at this hour?" he asked.

"We hope to do some good 'strafing,' sir," said the subaltern. "I'm coming up to observe. Some aeroplane fellow has found out that Brother Boche does his relieving by day in the trenches opposite. We hope to catch the relief to-day at ten."

"Where are you going to observe from?"

"There's an old sniper's post in one of the trees just behind your trenches. If I get up there before light I shall get a topping view, and am not likely to get spotted. That's why I'm going up there now, before it gets light."

"Well, are you going to stick up on that confounded perch until ten o'clock?" asked the C.O. "You'd better come and have some breakfast with us first."

But the Observing Officer knew the necessity of getting to his post as soon as possible and, reluctantly refusing the Colonel's invitation, he went on his way. Ten minutes later, he was lying full length on a platform constructed in one of the trees just behind the firing line. With the aid of his glasses, he scanned the German sandbags and, in the growing light, picked out a broad communicating trench winding towards the rear. "Once they are in that gutter," he muttered, "we shall get lots of them," and he allowed this thought to fortify him during his long wait.

"Quite sure the telephone's all right?" asked the Observing Officer for the fiftieth time. "If that wire were to go wrong we should have no means of getting on to the battery, for the infantry can only get on by 'phoning to Brigade Headquarters first, and you know what that means."

The telephone orderly, situated in a trench almost underneath the observer's tree, smiled consolingly, "That's all right, sir," he said. "I can ring up the battery in a second when the 'Uns come, as they ought to in a minute."

He had hardly spoken when they came. The subaltern could see them quite distinctly at the turnings of the trench, and at other times an occasional head or rifle showed itself. "God!" said the subaltern, "if we search that trench with shrapnel, we must get heaps of them," and he issued a hurried order. Trembling in his excitement, he awaited the report "Just fired, sir," but nothing happened. The orderly called and called the battery, but there was no reply. The wire was cut!

Half an hour later, the Battery Major came across his Observing Officer and a sergeant gazing dismally at two ends of cut wire.

"I was just coming down to see what was the matter. I hear from the Brigade that some doddering idiot has cut our wire. Who in the hell was it?"

"I don't know, sir. All I know is that I have seen a wonderful target, and couldn't fire a round at it. The relief's over by now, and, as we leave this sector to-night, we've lost a priceless chance."

"It must be some wretched infantry blighter," said the Major. "I'll just go and have a talk to their C.O.," and he hurried off to the Colonel's dug-out, leaving the Observer to lament his lost target.

The C.O. smiled soothingly. "My dear Wilson," he said to the Major, "I don't think it could have been one of our men. They have been warned so often. What do you say, Richards?" he asked the Adjutant.

"Well, sir, I'm not sure. I saw that young fellow Smith with some wire about half an hour ago, but I don't expect he did it. I'll send for him to make sure."

Second Lieutenant Archibald Smith certainly looked harmless enough. He was thin and freckled, and his big blue eyes gazed appealingly through his glasses.

"Where did you get that wire you had just now?" asked the Adjutant.

Smith beamed. "I got it just behind the wood, sir. There's a lot of old wi ..." but the Major interrupted him. "That's the place," he cried excitedly. "Well, what the devil did you go cutting my wire for?"

Archibald Smith looked at him in alarmed fascination. "I didn't think it was any good, sir. I wa-wanted some string, and...."

"What did you want string for? Were you going to hang yourself to the roof of your dug-out?"

"No, sir. I wanted to wrap up a p-parcel to send home, sir. I wa-anted to send back some socks and underclothes to be darned. I'm very sorry, sir."

"Sorry? Sorry be damned, and your underclothes too!" And the Battery Major, who had more bad language at his disposal than most men in the Army, for once forgot he was in the presence of a senior officer.

While the Major, his subaltern, and three men with a roll of wire wended their sorry way back to the battery, Archibald Smith, surprised and hurt, sat in his dug-out, amusing himself by making fierce bayonet thrusts at his parcel, and alternately wishing it were the Major or himself.

XXIV

THE NIGHTLY ROUND

I swear, and rub my eyes.

"Dusk, sir," says the Sergeant-Major with a smile of comprehension, and he lets fall the waterproof sheet which acts as a door to my dug-out. I yawn prodigiously, get up slowly from my bed—one of two banks of earth that run parallel down each side of my muddy hovel, rather after the fashion of seats down each side of an omnibus—and go out into the trench, along which the command "Stand to arms" has just been passed. The men leave their letters and their newspapers; Private Webb, who earned his living in times of peace by drawing thin, elongated ladies in varying stages of undress for fashion catalogues, puts aside his portrait of the Sergeant, who is still smiling with ecstasy at a tin of chloride of lime; the obstinate sleepers are roused, to a great flow of bad language, and all stand to their arms in the possibility of an attack.

It is a monotonous time, that hour of waiting until darkness falls, for gossip is scarce in the trenches, and the display of fireworks in the shape of German star shells has long since ceased to interest us—always excepting those moments when we are in front of our trench on some patrol. Away to the left, where the artillery have been busy all day, the shelling slackens as the light fades, and the rifle shots grow more and more frequent. Presently the extra sentries are posted—one man in every three—the disgusted working parties are told off to their work of filling sandbags or improving the communication trenches, and the long, trying night begins.

All down the line the German bullets spin overhead or crack like whips against our sandbags, sending little clods of earth down into the trench; all down the line we stand on our firing platforms, and answer back to the little spurts of flame which mark the enemy trench; sudden flashes and explosions tell of bombs or grenades, and star shells from both sides sweep high into the air to silhouette the unwary and to give one something to fire at, for firing into the darkness with the probability of hitting nothing more dangerous than a tree or a sandbag is work of but little interest.

I wander on my rounds to see that all the sentries are on the alert, and, suddenly, nearly fall over a man lying face downwards along the bottom of the trench. "Here, you can't sleep here, you know; you give no one a chance to pass," I say, and, for answer, I am told to "shut up," while a suppressed but still audible giggle from Private Harris warns me that the situation is not as I had imagined. The figure in the mud gets up and proves to be an officer of the Engineers, listening for sounds of mining underneath us. "I think they're at it again, but I'm not certain yet," he says cheerfully as he goes off to his own dug-out. I, in turn, lie down in the mud with my ear pressed to the ground, and I seem to hear, far beneath me, the rumble of the trolleys and the sound of the pick, so that I am left for the rest of the night in the uncomfortable expectation of flying heavenwards at any moment.

A buzz of voices which reaches me as I return from a visit to a working party informs me that the one great event of the night has taken place—the rations and the mail have arrived and have been "dumped" by the carrying party in a little side trench. Before I reach the spot a man comes hurrying up to me, "Please, sir," he says, "young Denham has been hit by a rifle grenade. 'E's got it very bad." Just as I pass the side trench, I hear the sergeant who is issuing the letters call: "Denham. A letter for young Denham," and someone says, "I'll take it to him, Sergeant, 'e's in my section."
But the letter has arrived too late, for when I reach the other end of the trench Denham is dead, and a corporal, is carefully searching his pockets for his letters and money to hand over to the platoon commander. They have carried him close to the brazier for light, and the flames find reflection on the white skin of his throat where his tunic has been torn open, and there is an ugly black stain on the bandage that has been roughly tied round him. Only one man in millions, it is true, but one more letter sent home with that awful "Killed" written across it, and one more mother mourning for her only child.
And so the night draws on. Now there is a lull, and the sentries, standing on the fire platforms, allow their heavy lids to fall in a moment's sleep; now a sudden burst of intense fire runs along the line, and everyone springs to his rifle, while star shells go up by dozens; now a huge rumble from the distance tells that a mine has been fired, and we wonder dully who fired it, and how many have been killed—dully only, for death has long since ceased to mean anything to us, and our powers of realisation and pity, thank God! have been blunted until the only things that matter are food and sleep.
At last the order to stand to arms is given again, and the new day comes creeping sadly over the plain of Flanders. What looked like a great hand stretched up appealingly to heaven becomes a shattered, broken tree; the uniform veil of grey gives place to grass and empty tins, dead bodies lying huddled up grotesquely, and winding lines of German trenches. The sky goes faintly blue, and the sun peeps out, gleaming on the drops of rain that still hang from our barbed wire, and on the long row of bayonets along the trench.

The new day is here, but what will it bring? The monotony may be broken by an attack, the battalion may be relieved. Who knows? Who cares? Enough that daylight is here and the sun is shining, that periscopes and sleep are once more permitted, that breakfast is at hand, and that some day we shall get back to billets.

XXV

JOHN WILLIAMS, TRAMP AND SOLDIER

On a wet and cheerless evening in September 1914, John Williams, tramp, sat in the bar of the Golden Lion and gazed regretfully at the tankard before him, which must of necessity remain empty, seeing that he had just spent his last penny. To him came a recruiting sergeant.

"Would you like a drink, mate?" he asked.

John Williams did not hesitate.

"You ought to be in the Army," said the sergeant, as he put down his empty tankard, "a fine great body of a man like you. It's the best life there is."

"I bean't so sartain as I want to be a sojer. I be a hindependent man."

"It's a good life for a healthy man," went on the sergeant. "We'll talk it over," and he ordered another drink apiece.

John Williams, who had had more than enough before the sergeant had spoken to him, gazed mistily at his new acquaintance. "Thee do seem to have a main lot o' money to spend."

The sergeant laughed. "It's Army pay, mate, as does it. I get a fine, easy life, good clothes and food, and plenty of money for my glass of beer. Where did you sleep last night?" he asked suddenly.

"If I do mind me right," said John Williams, "it were in a leaky barn, over Newton way."

"Where are you going to sleep to-night?" asked the sergeant again.

Williams remembered his empty pocket. "I doan't know," he said with regret. "Most likely on some seat in the park."

"Well, you come along o' me, and you'll get a comfortable barricks to sleep in, a life as you likes, and a bob a day to spend on yourself."

John Williams listened to the dripping of the rain outside. To his bemused brain the thought of a "comfortable barricks" was very, very tempting. "Blame me if I doan't come along o' thee," he said at length.

In wartime a medical examination is soon over and an attestation paper filled up. "There's nothing wrong with you, my man," said the Medical Officer, "except that you're half drunk."

"I bean't drunk, mister," protested Williams sleepily.

"We'll take you at your word, anyhow," said the doctor. "You're too good a man physically to lose for the Army."

Thus it was that John Williams took the King's Shilling, and swore to serve his country as a soldier should.

One of the most wonderful things about the British Army is the way that recruits are gradually fashioned into soldiers. There are thousands of men fighting on our different fronts who, a year ago, hated the thought of discipline and order; they are now amongst the best soldiers we have. But there are exceptions—Private John Williams was one. In a little over a year of military service, he had absented himself without leave no fewer than eleven times, and the various punishments meted out to him failed signally in their object to break him of his habit. In every respect save one he was a good soldier, but, do what it would, the Army could not bring him to see the folly of repeated desertion; the life in the Army is not the life for a man with the wander thirst of centuries in his blood. Williams had all the gipsy's love of wandering and solitude, and not even a threatened punishment of death will cure a man of that.

So it came about that John Williams sat outside his billet one September evening, and watched the white chalk road that ran over the hill towards Amiens. After the flat and cultivated country of Flanders, the rolling hills called with an unparalleled insistence, and the idea of spending the two remaining days before the battalion went back to the trenches in company with sixty other men in a barn grew more and more odious. If he were to go off even for twenty-four hours, he would receive, on return, probably nothing more than a few days Field Punishment, which, after all, was not so bad when one grew used to it. He was sick of the life of a soldier, sick of obeying officers half his age, sick of being ordered to do things that seemed senseless to him; he would be quit of it all for twenty-four hours.

John Williams went to the only shop in the village to buy food, with the aid of fifty centimes and a wonderful Lingua Franca of his own, and when his companions collected in their billet that night he was already far away on the open road. He walked fast through the still September evening, and as he walked he sang, and the woods echoed to the strange songs that gipsies sing to themselves as they squat round their fires at night. When at last he came to a halt he soon found sleep, and lay huddled up in his greatcoat at the foot of a poplar tree, until the dawn awoke him.

All through the summer day he walked, his Romany blood singing in his veins at the feel of the turf beneath his feet, and evening found him strolling contentedly through the village to his billet. Suddenly a sentry challenged: "'Alt! who goes there?"

"Downshires," came the reply.

"Well, what the 'ell are you doin' of 'ere?"

"I be going back to my regiment."

"Well, your regiment's in the trenches. They relieved us sudden like last night, owing to us getting cut up. You see, they Germans attacked us and killed a good few of our chaps before we drove 'em out again, so the Downshires 'ad to come up and relieve us late; somewhere about eleven o'clock they must 'ave left 'ere. What are you doing of, any'ow?" he asked jokingly. "Are you a bloomin' deserter what's come to be arrested?" But he posed the question to empty air, for Williams was retracing his steps at a steady double.

"Seems to me that bloke 'll get hisself inter trouble," said the sentry of the Westfords as he spat in disgust. Then he forgot all about it, and fell to wondering what the bar of the Horse and Plough must be looking like at the moment.

John Williams knew that he had burnt his boats, and he became a deserter in real earnest. For several weeks he remained at large, and each day made the idea of giving himself up of his own accord more difficult to entertain; but at last he was singled out from among the many men who wander about behind the firing line, and was placed under a guard that put hope of escape out of the question. Not even the wander thirst in his gipsy blood could set his feet on the wide chalk road again, or give him one more night of freedom.

"He might have a long term of imprisonment, mightn't he, sir?" asked the junior member of the Court Martial. "He could have no idea that his regiment was suddenly warned for the trenches when he deserted. Besides, the man used to be a tramp, and it must be exceptionally hard for a man who has led a wandering life to accustom himself to discipline. It must be in his blood to desert." And he blushed slightly, for he sounded sentimental, and there is little room for sentiment in an army on active service.

The President of the Court was a Major who liked his warm fire and his linen sheets, which, with the elements of discipline and warfare, occupied most of his thoughts. "I fear you forget," he said rather testily, "that this is the twelfth occasion on which this man has made off. I have never heard of such a case in my life. Besides, on this occasion he was warned that the Downshires were in the trenches by the sentry of the Westfords, and, instead of giving himself up, he deliberately turned round and ran off, so that the excuse of ignorance does not hold water. That the man was a tramp is, to my mind, no excuse either—the army is not a rest home for tired tramps. The man is an out-and-out scoundrel."

So the junior member, fearful of seeming sentimental and unmilitary, timidly suggested the sentence of death, to which the other two agreed.

"We must make an example of these fellows. There are far too many cases of desertion," said the Major, as he lit his pipe and hurried off to his tea.

Thus ended the career of No. 1234 Pte. John Williams, formerly a tramp in the west of England, unmourned and despised.

On the morning after he had been shot, his platoon sergeant sat before a brazier and talked to a corporal. "'E ain't no bloomin' loss, 'e ain't. 'E gave me too much trouble, and I got fair sick of 'aving to report 'im absent. It serves 'im blamed well right, that's what I say."

The corporal sipped his tea out of an extremely dirty canteen. "Well," he said at length, "I 'ope as the poor devil don't find it so warm where 'e's gone as what it is 'ere. I quite liked un, though 'e were a bit free with 'is fists, and always dreamin' like," which was probably the only appreciation ever uttered in memory of John Williams, tramp and soldier.

XXVI

THE CLEARING HOUSE

You collect your belongings, you stretch and yawn, you rub your eyes to rid them of sleep—and incidentally you leave great black marks all down your face—you struggle to get on your equipment in a filthy second-class carriage where are three other officers struggling to get on their equipment, and waving their arms about like the sails of windmills. Then you obtain a half share of the window and gaze out as the train crawls round the outskirts of the town, that lies still and quiet in the dusk of the morning. You have arrived at your destination—you are at the base.

This quaint old town, with its streets running up the hill from the river, with its beautiful spires and queer old houses, is the great clearing house of the British Army. Here the new troops arrive; here they leave for the front; here, muddy and wounded, they are driven in motor chars-à-bancs and ambulances from the station to the hospitals; here they are driven down to the river-side and carried on to the hospital ships that are bound for England.

And this gigantic clearing house buzzes with soldiers in khaki. There are the hotels where the generals and staff officers take their tea; there are the cafés haunted by subalterns; there are little "Débits de Vins" where "Tommies" go and explain, in "pidgin" English, that they are dying for glasses of beer. In all the streets, great motor lorries lumber by, laden with blackened soldiers who have been down on the quay, unloading shells, food, hay, oil, anything and everything that can be needed for the British Expeditionary Force. And, in the two main thoroughfares of an afternoon, there flows an unceasing crowd—generals and privates, French men and women, officers hunting through the shops for comforts to take up the line, people winding their busy way through the throng, and people strolling along with the tide, intent on snatching all they can of pleasure and amusement while they have the opportunity.

And a few years ago these same streets would lie sleepily in the sun, dreaming of the days of splendour long by. In the square before the wonderful cathedral there would be stillness—here and there, perhaps, a pigeon would come fluttering down from the ledges and cornices of the Gothic façade; sometimes a nondescript dog would raise a lazy head to snap at the flies; occasionally the streets would send back a nasal echo as a group of American tourists, with their Baedekers and maps, came hurrying along to "do" the town before the next train left for Paris—beyond that ... nothing.

Now, in the early morning, the Base seems almost to have relapsed into its slumber of yore. As yet, the work of the day has not begun, and the whole town seems to stir sleepily as the screeching brakes bring your train to a standstill. As you stumble out of the carriage, the only living person in the place appears to be a sentry, who tramps up and down in the distance, on guard over a few empty trucks and a huge pile of bundles of straw.

It is a little disappointing, this arrival at the Base, for there is not even a proper station in sight; you have been brought, like so many sheep or cows, into the dismal goods station, and you look in vain for the people who should be there to welcome you, to throw flowers, and to cheer as you arrive at the first halt of your great Odyssey. However, you shake yourself, you bundle your valise out of the carriage on to the railway line, and, with your late carriage companions, you go across to the sentry and his bundles of straw.

"Can you tell us where the Railway Transport Officer is to be found?" you ask. "We've got orders to report to him as soon as we can."

"Yes, sir, they's always got those orders, but you won't find 'im not before 'alf-past nine. 'Is office is over there in them buildings." And a subaltern in the office gives you the same information—it is now five o'clock, and the R.T.O. who has your movement orders will not be here for four and a half hours. "Go and have a look round the town," suggests the subaltern.

The idea of "looking round a town" at five in the morning! You slouch over the bridge, and wander up and down the empty streets until an hotel shows up before you. You are very tired and very dirty and very unshaven. Instinctively you halt and feel your chins. "Dunno when we'll get another bath," suggests one of the party, and he goes to ring the bell. For ten minutes you ring the bell, and then the door is opened by a half-clothed porter who is also very tired and very dirty and very unshaven. He glares at you, and then signs to you to enter, after which he runs away and leaves you in a hall in the company of a dust pan and brush and a pile of chairs pushed up in the corner—no welcome and no flowers.

But in a moment there is a shuffle on the stairs, and a fat, buxom woman, with a cheerful face and a blouse undone down the back, makes her appearance. Oh yes, Messieurs les Officiers can have a bath—for two francs, including a towel; and they can have breakfast—for three and a half francs, including "ze English marmalade" and "un œuf à la coque" (which sets you to wondering whether she means a cock's egg, and, if so, what sort of a thing it may be). "It is a nice bath," she tells you, "and always full of Messieurs les Anglais, who forget all about the war and only think of baths and of football. No, zere is only one bath, but ze ozer officiers can wait," and she leads one of the party away into the dim corridors and up dim staircases.

Breakfast and a wash work wonders, and you still keep cheerful when the R.T.O. tells you at half-past nine that your camp is three miles away, that you may not see your valise for days unless you take a "taxi," and that there are only three "taxis" in the town. You wander about in search of one during the whole morning, you find the three all hiding away together in a side street, you bundle your valises into one, and arrive at the camp just in time for lunch.

It is a strange life, that life at the Base—it is like life on an "island" in a London thoroughfare, with the traffic streaming by on either side. All day long there are men arriving to go to the front, all day long there are men coming back on their way to England. For a week you live on this "island," equipping men for drafts all the morning—for most of them seem to have dropped part of their equipment into the sea on the way across—and sitting in cafés in the evenings, drinking strange mixtures of wines and syrups and soda water.

Then, one day, the Colonel sends for you. Your turn has come to set out on that journey which may have no return. "You will proceed to the front by the four o'clock train this afternoon," he says. "You are instructed to conduct a party of 100 Northshire Highlanders, who are in 'S' Camp, which is over there," and he waves his hand vaguely in the direction of the typewriter in the corner of the room.

These are your instructions, and, after a prolonged hunt for "S" Camp, you march off to the station at the head of a hundred Scotchmen, not one of whom you can understand. At the station you make a great show of nominal rolls and movement orders, and finally get your Highlanders packed safely in their compartments under strict injunctions not to leave the train without your orders.

Now comes the time to look after your own comfort. If you have "been up" before you have learnt that it is wise to stroll into the town for your last proper tea, and not to come back much before six o'clock, by which time the train is thinking of reluctantly crawling out of the station. If, in your absence, someone has else has tried to settle in your compartment, providing his rank is not superior to your own, you get rid of him either by lying strenuously or by using a little force. Thus, if you are lucky, a good liar, or a muscular man, you can keep the carriage for yourself, your particular friend, your kits, and your provisions (which last, in the form of bottles, require no small space).

All along the line are children, waving their grubby hands and shouting in monotonous reiteration, "Souvenir biskeet, souvenir bully biff," and you throw them their souvenirs without delay, for no man sets out for war without a plentiful stock of more interesting provisions to keep his spirits up. All along the train, in disobedience of orders, the carriage doors are open, and "Tommies" and "Jocks," and "Pats" are seated on the footboards, singing, shouting, laughing.

This, until night falls. Then, one by one, the carriage doors are shut, and the men set about the business of sleeping. Here and there, perhaps, is a man who stays awake, wondering what the future will bring him, how his wife and children will get on if he is killed, and how many of these men, who are lolling in grotesque attitudes all round him, will ever come back down the line. In the daylight, the excitement drives away these thoughts—there are songs to sing and sights to see—but as the train jolts on through the night, there seems to be an undefinable feeling of fear. What will it be like to be shelled, to fight, to die?

Morning brings cheerfulness again. There are halts at Boulogne and Calais; news must be obtained from English sentries and French railway officials; there is, in one place, a train of German prisoners; there are long halts at tiny stations where you can procure hot water while the O.C. Train discusses life with the R.T.O.; there are the thousand-and-one things which serve to remind you that you are in the war zone, although the country is peaceful, and you look in vain for shell holes and ruined houses.

At length the railhead is reached—from here the rumble of the guns can be heard—and the detrainment takes place. You fall your Highlanders in by the side of the train, you jerk your pack about in a vain effort to make it hang comfortably, a whistle blows, and you start off on your long march to your regiment, to those dull, mumbling guns, to your first peep of war.

A "cushy" wound, a long and aching journey in a motor ambulance, a nerve-racking night in a clearing hospital, where the groans of the dying, the hurrying of the orderlies, and your own pain all combine in a nightmare of horror, and next morning you are in the train once more—you are going back to the Base. But how different is this from the journey up to the front! The sound of distant firing has none of the interest of novelty; the shelling of an aeroplane, which would have filled you with excitement a short time ago, does not now even cause you to raise your eyes to watch; you are old in warfare, and *blasé*.

There is no room for fear on this train; it is crowded out by pain, by apathy, by hope. The man next you cannot live a week, but he seems content; at all events, it is not fear that one sees in his face. There is no fear—there is hope.

The train is bright with flowers; there are nurses, and books, and well-cooked food—there is even champagne for the select few. There is no longer the shattered country of the firing line, but there are hills and rivers, there is the sea near Wimereux, and the hope of being sent home to England. There are shattered wrecks that were men, there is the knowledge of hovering death, but, above all, there is hope.

So the train hastens on—no crawling this time—to the clearing house, the Base. Past the little sun-washed villages it runs, and the gleaming Seine brings smiles to wan faces. There, look, over there in the distance, are the wonderful spires and the quaint houses and the river, all fresh and laughing in the sun, and the trees up on the hill above the town are all tender green. Even if one is to die, one may get back home first; at all events, one has been spared to see God's clean country, and to breathe untainted air again.

9 789357 959476